THE UGLY BEAUTIFUL PEOPLE

ESSAYS ON LIBERAL CULTURE BY LEOPOLD TYRMAND

UNIVERSITY PRESS OF AMERICA,™ INC.

LANHAM • NEW YORK • LONDON

Copyright © 1985 by Leopold Tyrmand

University Press of America,™ Inc.

4720 Boston Way
Lanham. MD 20706

3 Henrietta Street
London WC2E 8LU England

Library of Congress Cataloging in Publication Data

Tyrmand, Leopold.
    The ugly beautiful people.

    1. United States—Popular culture—History—20th
century—Addresses, essays, lectures. 2. United States—
Civilization—1945- —Addresses, essays, lectures.
3. Liberalism—United States—History—20th century—
Addresses, essays, lectures. 4. Civilization, Modern—
1950- —Addresses, essays, lectures. I. Title.
E169.12.T95   1984   973.9   84-20972
ISBN 0-8191-4086-4 (alk. paper)
ISBN 0-8191-4143-7 (pbk. : alk. paper)

All University Press of America books are produced on acid-free
paper which exceeds the minimum standards set by the National
Historical Publications and Records Commission.

To Mary Ellen, my wife—

Acknowledgments

Most of this book has seen print in various publications of the Rockford Institute. Thus, the opinions expressed here do not differ from those published in *The Rockford Papers* or *Chronicles of Culture*.

In conceptualizing and formulating many of those views, I am indebted to the Institute's president, Dr. John A. Howard, his faithfulness and rectitude.

I am grateful to Mrs. Rebecca Woosley, former managing editor of the *Chronicles*, for her aid in bringing cohesiveness to a volume that consists of so many disparate trials.

Table of Contents

Introduction

This book consists of pamphlets, speeches, and editorials which were published in the *Chronicles of Culture* between 1978 and 1982. Pamphleteering is common to each of these genres. It is their substance, their message, their goal.

Our age of spiritual unrest and moral confusion requires a return to the tradition of expressing concern and judgment independent of the powerful centers of opinion. A giant idea-forming industry proclaims impartiality a virtue. But expedient evenhandedness often results in listless objectivity which, in turn, becomes a breeding ground for indifference, helplessness and cynicism. Whoever attempts to pursue truth cannot and will not be impartial. In his endeavors, he must begin with a set of moral principles which he sees as just, correct and valid, if he intends to defend them and wants to interpret what is around him in accord with his sense of good and bad. This is, perhaps, why the time-honored, personal, value-oriented art of pamphleteering is making a remarkable comeback. If convictions are presented in a way that emanates integrity and commitment, and conveys intellectual effort and persuasive reasoning, they sooner or later induce change. The history of the Western world has proved it.

In a world where various forces are attempting to effect change by various means, one's best hope is to be in the forefront of change through ideas. The idea of reviving allegiance to individual responsibility within the framework of a free society seems to be of paramount importance. The printed word was for centuries the most efficient carrier of ideas. However, in an era when books often have the life span of a daily newspaper, and newspapers do not care about sustaining a durable identity, it is difficult to restore the printed word's promise and influence. Yet to one who trusts that it is within human reach to discern right from wrong by dint of mind and heart—it's the only way.

CHAPTER 1

Two Cultures*

I am occasionally reminded (some would say warned), by people whom I respect, that my polemical tone carries a seed of zealotry. This may result, say those who remind me, in unreflective rejections. If this is the case, I must have misguided my messages, as narrow partisanship was never my ambition. I do not want to become a cause of showdowns, in either word or deed. But I do want to stir intellectual emotions.

We all feel that the divisions of the last two decades must be defined in ideological categories. The liberal/conservative dichotomy befits those categories. These days, a liberal is one who has no qualms in accepting that everything around him is deteriorating into what he sees as a better world. The conservative stands aghast at the sight of everything improving for the worse. Along these lines of confusion, there is emerging a rift between two American cultures which may determine the future of this country.

Such duality was noticed long ago by the Greeks—the inventors of both democracy and snobbery, plebeian sloganeering and cultural sophistication. Ever since, sages and socialites have been talking about culture and folklore, court culture and the vulgar one, high- and low-brow, pop or mass culture. To be true, the Middle Ages witnessed a situation when an intense Christianity transcended borderlines and different tastes: Gregorian chants moved to tears the feudal squire and his serfs alike; both the lowborn and the knight admired Giotto, Cimabue and the Chartres Cathedral. Thereafter, the dual cultural pattern was delineated at the peak of the Renaissance by Castiglione in *The Courtier*, and from then on it has been susceptible to ambivalences and perversions. Early romanticism fed on folk legends only to fashion attitudes of modish melancholy quite alien to the bustling reality of folksy capitalism. Karl Marx turned his socioeconomic teachings into a moral proposition; it was soon transformed into a morality play, and as such is still staged in the Central Park West salons of the wealthy. Bertolt Brecht and René Clair created great art from proletarian street ballads, only to contribute to the highbrow cultural soufflé, though it would be unfair to claim that its consumption was limited to millionaires' drawing rooms. Abstract painting found its way onto Woolworth's neckties. D. H. Lawrence, a coal miner's son, wished to speak about the conscience of the common Englishman, only to become the minion of literary gourmets. Today, with television in almost every American household, the demierudite tube priests daily convey highbrow concepts, dry-roasted and pre-packaged according to the liberal recipe. Truckers debate Freud and Sartre in turnpike diners without even knowing it, Mahler is passed on to the masses via movie scores, and telephone installers look as if they have just come from Vidal Sasson. The ideological ivory towers of the modern court culture became social conscience and revolution: dreams about utopian justice achieved through violence, upheaval and blood in the gutters remain the single exclusivity which the masses have left to the literati and cognoscenti. If the contemporary American farmer and worker is quite able to acculturate himself to every fad and antic of the establishment, the one he refuses to ape is the establishment's ravenous appetite for fuzzy idealism at someone else's expense, one that is rooted in self-hatred, neuroses and psychic debilitations.

Court culture was not always radical; most often it was supercilious, exclusive, contemptuous or just enamored with dimwitted mendacities, like bergerettes in the Petit Trianon. The last 200 years have been a variety of oddities: 18th-century Jacobin bankers from New York City, 19th-century populist terrorists of patrician wealth from Massachusetts, Anita McCormick Blaine from Chicago squandering the International Harvester fortune to support Henry Wallace and communist papers, and the latest California "radical chic" which makes pro-communist stars and movie moguls pour their millions into the cultural advance machine for revolution. And the masses refuse to follow. The promiscuously fondled social conscience reached its climax in the 1960's on the infamous cover of the *New York Review of Books*—an organ of highbrow cultural elitism: it featured a diagram for how to make a Molotov cocktail for the benefit of the liberal establishment's sons and daughters at Ivy League schools who might have felt like bombing a bank or a precinct. Thereby, the court culture of the USA has reached a degeneracy known to other ages, but never so sordid as it is now. Its decay was hastened by journalistic maggots who permeated the new pop-mass-cultural amalgam of the 70's with venom and insanity—when a letter to the editor could begin, in all seriousness: "I am a normal 19-year-old bisexual woman . . ."

Not long ago, Lord Snow declared that court/elite culture versus folk/pop culture is an ancient story, whereas the duality now posits science against the humanities. Mathematicians of genius know all about the metaphysics of nuclear physics but have never read Kafka. This has its cause in the effort necessary for specialization in our epoch. But I doubt that this conditions the dichotomous reality in which we live, and, whether we like it or not, we must call the two opposing cultures liberal and conservative. The crucial questions therefore are: What are their similarities and differences? Where is the epicenter of cultural power in today's America? Who holds the levers? How are the gears operated?

These are difficult questions to answer. Gulf & Western is a mammoth corporation which should stand for capitalism, profits and a free market. Yet its subsidiaries—publishing houses, record companies, Paramount Pictures —publish books, sell albums and make movies which present capitalism as Satan's invention and openly desire its instant demise. This is nothing extraordinary, as Gulf & Western is also a *liberal* conglomerate, whose leaders believe in culture as a stock exchange of ideas where values should float freely and win or lose according to the laws of the market. Under these conditions, cultural commodities earn money—and Gulf & Western is primarily interested in money. Since social conscience is the foremost money-making proposition these days, economy and ethics happily readjust one another in Gulf & Western's board-room philosophy, and no spiritual conflict threatens the minds of its top managers. Now, there are many corporate giants which are both utterly liberal and into culture. Together with the liberal eminentos, they form the liberal cultural establishment. Whether their opposition is either organized religion or a solitary American who believes that culture (and its sway over daily life) should be value-oriented and related to our heritage, the outcome of the power game is quite obvious. The liberal culture just engulfs the American culture.

Which, of course, means suppression of the adversary culture. Suppression? In democratic America, where everybody can, thanks to the First Amendment, express his views? No one prohibits anybody from publishing a book, making a movie, launching a TV station. That's true, but in our technotronic reality, an idea, a defense of a value, or an alternate view is not a matter of expression but of visibility, audibility, dissemination. The media are the modern passkey to human consciousness and they are overwhelmingly dedicated to the liberal culture. That is—the media are committed body and soul to the idea of progress toward an endlessly inferior world. The liberals, proud of their nonconformism, have rebelled against hypocrisy over the centuries; their rebellion has become an orthodoxy and anybody who *now* rebels against their cant is hypocritically branded a bigot and made the object of either ridicule or stony silence, as the official stand of the liberal culture is that its adversary is culturally inferior. The liberal worldview *only* is declared respectable, and the culture engendered by it auspicious, wise, worthy of attention. But is that so? Even if conservatives and traditionalists may command the allegiance of more minds and souls in America (and we don't know if that is the case, since the pollsters are reluctant to let conservative scholars formulate their questionnaires), the media will always make it invisible. They know how to do it;* they are masters of tokenism, so they fraudulently reduce the conservative cultural force to a handful of names. Why is it that the only opinion on hard-working small businessmen comes from Burbank, or Manhattan, where smart alecks are making fortunes by turning the moral satisfactions of decent hard work into a rat race by means of derisive one-liners? Every reader of newspapers knows that Goldwater is a conservative, but nobody knows that Faulkner was our greatest conservative writer. We are sternly

---

Time magazine, for instance, refuses to print, in its "Letters to the Editor" column, any intelligent rebuff of its liberal biases, favoring, instead, inarticulate and doltish ones, giving them an instant yahoo imprint by innuendo.

instructed by the press and show biz that love is a liberal idea, and faithfulness a conservative one, but to prove that love is ennobled by faithfulness is forbidden. By preaching anticapitalism and chintzy hedonism in the same breath, the liberal culture has lost any title to the moral representation of hard-working, law-abiding, normalcy-and-common-sense-craving America. However, the near monopoly of cultural means and the quasi-totalitarian method of ignoring voices of protest present only the liberal image of the reality.

Which makes the two-culture syndrome in America a system of oppression and abuse. To some, it may seem amusing that punk rock, with all its beastly imbecility, is the plaything of the court culture, while the music of Boston Pops serves the plain folk. These paradoxes are at the core of social aberrations. The pristine conviction that social and cultural power are still in the hands of the old financial establishment is an illusion. The cultural, thus the political, standards are now ordained by what some call the New Class. In the early 50's, plenty of brainy and fiercely liberal, if not outrightly radical-minded people, scared stiff by McCarthy, went from politics into professions—journalism, theater, labor law, publishing, etc. Within two decades, they had monopolized the opinion-making apparatus of the country and gathered fabulous wealth along the way. But their allegiances remained the same, and today a mining tycoon is financing the Institute for Policy Studies, an overtly procommunist research center. Professions whose social basis was the bohemian left (stage setting, fashion photography, sound engineering, etc.) have become sources of financial opulence for left-wing politics. The critics of the New Class locate its members mostly in the academe, bureaucracy, the media; but what about the weight of all that money for left causes that comes from the superaffluent Hollywood cameramen or radical disc jockeys?

Some time ago one could read in the *New York Times Book Review* that *now* ideas matter, that intellectual movements are *now* influencing politics. But hasn't it always been so? Didn't ideas always generate political events, only in slower sequence than in the era of Telex and communication satellites? Aren't the TV anchormen and press editorialists just the tom-toms of the idea producer, only quicker in transmitting the watchword to immense audiences? The highbrow culture enamored by radicalism has been a particular beneficiary of this rapid change.

This brings me to perhaps the fundamental difference between *their* culture and *mine*. Great art, poetry, music, literature comes from the struggle against the real enemies of mankind: death, misfortune, cruelty, ignorance, insanity, political conquest and subjugation. It never originates in bantering with minor afflictions, discomforts, boredoms, frustrations, artificially inflated social "sufferings." An epoch, in which there's no fight for that which touches the soul of the common folk, engenders a minor culture which mirrors trivia and whose reflections are easily forgotten. When contention is moot because everything is permitted, no creativity flourishes. A reigning culture that pushes books which are nothing but extensions of newspapers is inferior; this—when faced with cultural propositions that speak of moral discipline—it must crush the latter's superiority by totalitarian means. When Pope John Paul II, who clearly belongs to the contemporary nonliberal culture, preaches antiviolence and antipoverty but culls his spiritual force from principle, tradition, fidelity to canon, he must be denounced, for he proves that humane goals and progress can be found in a conservative impulse. Every ruling set of values which upholds its unassailability by administrative and bureaucratic means begins to rot first in arts and letters—precisely because they are privileged and protected. The liberals in America have not yet attained the Soviet style of protectionism, but a special tariff for the liberal twaddle became a rule of cultural life in America in the 60's and 70's. The Vidals, Mailers, Vonneguts, the Hollywood radical cinema may be only occasionally and mildly admonished by the liberal interpreters, but never meaningfully criticized, dissected, evaluated. Their formal shortcomings may be pointed out, their philosophy—never. No one may ask what the Cheevers, Styrons, Hellers, et al. have ever given to America, to mankind, to their fellow man— except for literary smartness, cynicism touted as inquiry, desperate manner- ism, pharisaical or sanctimonious depressiveness, lascivious pseudomelan- choly and modish etiolation of characters. The fertile Americanism of the Faulkners, Hemingways, Sinclair Lewises, O'Haras has been abandoned amidst the coquettish squeaks of self-hatred. The old naturalism used to proclaim: "Look how it really is! Isn't it terrible?"; the neonaturalism of the Irvings and Baldwins now says: "Look how it really is! Isn't it cute?" Hope, social dynamics, respect for the dignity and heroism of the other, indeed the entire democratic pluralism recedes before the onslaught of the neurotic phobias of the other and capitulates to the other's freakishness. No one knows any longer in whose name cultural facts are praised or condemned. If nonlib- eral critics condemn a Capote or a Roth, they know why they do it. But what are the liberal culture's normative criteria? In Time, Inc.'s in-house leaflet, we can find a clue to *Time* magazine's critical ethics, as its literary critic elucidates on the subject: " 'When I write,' he explains, 'it's just me and the book. I have two basic responsibilities to an author: to try to understand his purpose, and to evaluate how well he succeeds. The reviewer's third responsibility,' he adds, 'is to be absolutely clear and accessible to the reader.' " Thereby, the "critic" tells me that if he had to review Adolf Hitler's *Mein Kampf*, he would have praised it to the skies: Hitler's purpose was easily understandable, he perfectly succeeded in articulating his message, and *Time's* book appraiser would have had no trouble in conveying it clearly and accessibly to his readers. End of *Time* magazine book critic's responsibilities.

In contrast to the cultural ethos of *Time*, central to *my* culture is perman- ence and an orderly hierarchy of values. For instance: the individual's moral obligation and responsibility toward another person, community, society, nation, toward civilization and its laws, traditions, institutions. The immanence of human bonds in cultural facts is the norm of our judgment of those facts—ideas, trends, books, movies, intellectual inquiries, etc. These bonds are for me the source of mankind's two most precious concepts: freedom and human dignity. It seems to me rather evident that modern liberal ideas, as they are embodied in the culture engendered by them and created daily by the cultural production, are neither willing nor able to defend and sustain human dignity; about freedom, they mean something different than I do. During the 20th century, the idea of social equality celebrated countless triumphs: in America, for one, things once accessible only through birth, privilege or money—plenty of food, abundant leisure, factual political leverage—have become standard. But freedom and dignity were trampled in Auschwitz and in Gulags; and in the socially successful America, the vulgarization, depersonalization and dehumanization of private life nowadays reduce them both to mockery. Thus, the defense of freedom and human dignity has become the gist of the conflict between *their* culture and *mine*.

We all feel confused and benumbed, sensing the loss of the center on which we can safely hang our ideals, beliefs and preferences. We all feel the urge to defend ethical goods, we sense a sort of salvation—general and private—in upholding them; we vaguely realize that this salvation begins *there*, in the cultural climate, not in economics, politics or social solutions. Many do not understand the spiritual dimensions of our predicament: in the past, the average American was not confronted with this interpretation of his malaise; he used to leave it to schools, churches, political and social arrangements which were supposed to give him sloganlike explications. Then television, with its power of smirking insouciance, overshadowed them all. The average American does not realize that the breakdown of sexual conventions means not only that people can do to their bodies what they wish but that, sooner or later, it entails the collapse of everything built on rule, custom, tradition, even the social contract itself, that it ultimately cancels both human warmth and those bondings on which his sense of life rests.

So I am trying to express my protest by judging the other culture. Like every protest of those who are deliberately ignored, mine can also be denounced as shrill and overwrought. But is it? I do my best to debunk the false greatness fabricated by the liberal culture and now and then a good man or woman or thought, transmogrified into an icon by the omnipotent liberal establishment and sycophancy, gets hurt. But I do not fling unsubstantiated charges; I do not indulge in self-serving showiness; I do not desecrate anybody's symbols. I just respectfully disagree with my adversaries. Anything else would be incompatible with the most cherished precepts of *my* culture.

CHAPTER 2

Commentary*

Chronicles of Culture originated as a protest against the perversion of the American culture by something we call the liberal culture. The marvelous cultural pluralism of the American civilization, grounded in the time-honored persuasion that the other's point of view is our common asset, has been corrupted by liberal zealotry in pursuit of a monopoly on truth. About four years ago we at The Rockford Institute felt that something should be done to redress the wrongs inflicted upon intellectual tenets that for so long, and with such prodigious achievements, had governed the American ethos as it is reflected in the national culture. We founded a bimonthly. Soon it became clear that we had found both an audience and our own image. So we recently decided to redouble our efforts and to accelerate the distribution of what we think and believe. Thus, instead of making our beliefs readable six times per year, we will be doing it twice as frequently. So here, briefly restated, is what we believe in.

The liberal polity, as it was anticipated by its 18th- and 19th-century champions, encompassed many components that we could very much appreciate. And, in reality, it did so in many respects. It evolved some invaluable concepts—representative democracy, the rule of law, voluntary social order, functional pluralism in culture (chiefly in America), the humanitarian principle. Its notions of justice and compassion came from the Judeo-Christian moral sense. Western liberal society as we know it is the end result of diverse philosophical contentions, religious hopes, ideological sensibilities and schools of thinking—from the Enlightenment treatises to the programs of old American Whigs. Notwithstanding its political vicissitudes, its basic vocabulary remained the same. Words like civilization, reason, humanity, optimism, commerce, progress, self-reliance, enterprise, individualism, responsibility constituted its framework. We have no quarrel with these words, but from them grew a culture whose sacrosanct tenet, or secular worship, became an unbounded amorphous self-criticism which finally perverted both concepts and values, stultified them into caricatures, eradicated their commonsensical substance, reduced them—in our time—to the level of driveling nihilism. At the peak of its splendor—before the process of perversion set in—this culture was called the "bourgeois culture"; it thrived and enriched the societies that developed it. Then it extended lush privileges to those who declared that attempts to destroy it would henceforth be called art, or literature, or amusement, or free inquiry, and that's where the downward spiral began.

During the 1960's and 70's, we witnessed in America the deliberate and unabashed murder of the bourgeois culture perpetrated in the name of ideas and tenets which had been corrupted. What emerged in its stead we named the liberal culture—because misguided liberal sentiments must bear the responsibility for its existence. Since we had a very warm spot for the bourgeois culture at the time of its bloom—and we intensely disliked what had been proposed, or rather superimposed, to take its place—we began to publish this journal. We recognized that the liberal culture was actually digging the grave of our entire civilization, so we went to war.

Under what banner do we battle?

To put it succinctly, we fight beneath our own flag. Liberalism maintains nowadays that all it wants is a decent society ensuring justice and dignity for all—but so do we. Liberals say they want a polity that is responsive to human needs, that they desire material sufficiency for everybody—so do we. However, we have one stipulation: all these precious goods must come by *public* consent, not through prefabricated recipes concocted by theorists and enforced by politicians who know how to manipulate constituencies and interest groups to the detriment of a larger idea and a national entity. When liberals demand honest pluralism in culture, this is exactly what we want. But do liberals live up to their preachings? It is obvious that they long ago abandoned a pluralism based on *authentic* differences of views. By exerting a totalitarianlike grip on the opinion-forming industry, their apologists and critics are able to bar any truly opposing point of view from the pages of influential liberal journals that loudly proclaim *urbi et orbi* their pure and benign ideological nonpartisanship. Long gone is that kind of intellectual pluralism which predicated the Adams-Jefferson difference as a treasure of American political philosophy. Today, Adams's writing would run the risk of being rejected out of hand by any junior editor at any major publishing house, while Jefferson, in order to elaborate on his convictions in an atmosphere of uninhibited toleration, would need to obtain a fellowship grant from the American Enterprise Institute.

Culture is a crutch word; we use it to denote the production and distribution of ideas and images. Behind every, even the most vulgar, sitcom, there's an idea; from the sitcom comes an image. But where did the liberal culture come from? Did it originate in technology, in social transmutations? This is what *they* would have us believe. But culture is not the result of attitudes, it is their generator, producer, manufacturer, source. Cultures in history have prospered within a climate of contention, dissension and internal adversary forces —and vigorousness of the discourse. That ambiance does not exist in today's America. The dominance of the liberal culture is absolute in nature and totalitarian in method—especially when it comes to the distribution of images. Non-liberal thought is distorted by the firmly liberal communications media and presented as political, cultural, moral, even intellectual deviltry without the benefit of a fair hearing, without the chance for an honest exchange of views. There are countless editorial devices and stratagems which enable the leadership of the *New York Times* or CBS to present such a procedure as evenhandedness, an Olympian impartiality in the struggle of ideas, a benevolent wisdom that transcends ideological and cultural adversities. In reality it is the manipulative and merciless suppression of another point of view—which always happens to be a nonliberal one.

It appears that, in the near future, the crucial fight will be between world views and philosophies for the human mind. This struggle will certainly take place in America, and we intend to be there on the battlefield. What we will be standing against is a culture that has disintegrated the vocabulary of ideas of the old bourgeois culture, that has stultified notions on which humankind built its hopes over millennia, conventions that throughout history have made us and our lives better. This new culture has annihilated our cherished sensibilities and trampled their remains into the morass of modern existence. It is a culture in which new catechetic words reign: liberation, entitlement, self-realization. According to the current liberal gospel, women must be liberated from their womanhood, and anyone who asks for anything makes it politically legitimate by the mere process of asking, while the pinnacle of humanness is to be found in singles bars, or freakish potential-movement happenings, or on the psychoanalytical couch. It is a culture in which behavioral slime is considered the prime element of literature, lesbianism is seen as a natural law at Princeton University, compassion has become a social regulation, fashion magazines preach revolution, and traitors to their country are presented to youth as symbols of integrity. One consequence of this culture is that a vast segment of the population is forced to work hard to support a class of parasites, many of whom—thanks to economic priorities gone berserk — have turned their lives into a grotesque *Grand Guignol* of drugs and kinky crime and who provide their own troubadours with an offensive wealth. It is a culture in which a nurse earns less per year than a cretinous, unwashed rock singer spends on dope per day. For this culture we have nothing but the deepest contempt, and we want to make it known. In the 1930's a German antifascist by the name of Carl von Ossietzky, before he was tortured by the nazis in Dachau, addressed himself to his nation in one of his last warnings: "All I wish is for you to remember, I was against!" So are we, when we face the travesty of humanness and the humiliation of reason in America.

Our first four years have convinced us that there is an audience among the young American intelligentsia whose criteria for truth, reason and intellectual honesty have *not* been shaped by *Time* magazine, or *Rolling Stone's* poetry, or *Mother Jone's* jaded socialism—often written by the scions of corporate tycoons. We do not think that the acknowledged centers of antiliberalism have the correct answer to the cultural pogrom unleashed by the vast liberal spectrum which ranges from open Soviet stooges at the Washington, D.C. radical think tanks to the jaundiced anti-Americans of *The Nation* or *Village Voice* stripe to the pseudohumanitarian parrots of the left-wing Republican Party. *We* want to speak to that audience out there. This is why we will double the frequency of our commentary.

Notes On Liberal Culture*

I am repeatedly asked to explain what I mean by the term "liberal culture." The general impression is that whatever it means I do not like it. This is correct.

So before we venture into subtle reasoning on what is meant by what, it should be stated forcefully and unequivocally that liberalism and the liberal culture are not synonymous and are often at odds. Liberal culture is the result of what liberalism—a time-honored, well-meaning ideology of humanitarian non-restraint—has done in our epoch to and with culture as an agent of moral order. The progressive assimilation and identification of liberalism with the liberal culture is a disturbing and deplorable occurrence.

Liberalism has enriched mankind with everlasting values. Man and society are indebted to its moral merits. As an attitude built around the predisposition to freedom, inquiry and progress, it has accompanied the Judeo-Christian civilization since its dawn. As a philosophy, it began with the Renaissance, and reached a golden age in the XVIII century Enlightenment—thus becoming endemic to the very conception of American society and statehood. Hobbes, Locke, Montesquieu, Adam Smith, Jefferson, Kant, Goethe, de Tocqueville, Lord Acton, Stendhal and Cavour would not have objected to being called liberals in the initial sense of the word. John Stuart Mill completed the liberal philosophy, while Gladstone determined liberal politics. Western democracy of today is unthinkable without those men. We are fed on their thought and vision. We owe our sense of modern justice, of social community and equity to their liberalism.

With the apotheosis of Western liberalism at the end of the XIX century, there began to emerge a world of new anxieties eagerly and quickly seized upon for development into ideological doctrines. Much earlier, Marxism had rejected liberalism as "a bourgeois faith, a hollow, never fulfilled promise of democracy."

Many liberals—Matthew Arnold comes first to mind—began to feel an intellectual itch for something more than freedom, reason, individualism, responsibility and tolerance. The quest for new orthodoxies carried deep into our age, spawning cultural and political extremisms. Somehow, sometime, liberalism lost its marvelous clarity of purpose, its masterfully articulated necessity of moral order, grounded in the respect for the human mind and conscience. "Progress was all right once, but it went on too long," this old and artful saying sums it all up.

Liberalism has now been appropriated as the label for so many causes that it is taken for what it is not. The highly moral motivations of Locke and Adam Smith, or the sophistication of de Tocqueville, gave way to the Whig insensitivity in England and a laissez-faire voracity American-style. When Francois Guizot, the French statesman, proclaimed his famous "Enrichissez-vous!" in the 1840's it was understood in its proper context, for Guizot was a man of renowned, even self-righteous, integrity. Men, he believed, should individually strive for affluence through industry and enterprise, but never without a keen sense of the moral perils and moral obligations involved in such endeavors. Although flattened and warped, this precept survives in many capitalistic circles.

Guizot, the champion of bourgeois liberalism, would have difficulty recognizing as fellow liberals Senators Kennedy and McGovern, who believe that the state and the government—society's executive arms—should solve the problems of economic destiny for American citizens. Thomas Hobbes, that Nestor of liberal philosophers, who wrote: "…liberties depend on the silence of the law—" would have read with disbelief the *New York Times'* manifestos on how liberalism today means freeing people from misery and ignorance with the help of an omnipotent bureaucracy. Since the '30s, American liberalism, even while still committed to the freedom of property and enterprise, has come to mean a social-democratic solution to social ills. Its old preoccupation with grounding moral postulates in reason, empirical dialectics, and civic virtues— such as fairness of judgment, toleration of other views, respect for other people—seems to have vanished.

In the mid-60's—the nadir of the American culture to my mind—a new doctrinal interpretation of liberalism emerged. I believe it hostile to man, woman and child alike and incompatible with Western civilization as we inherited it from its builders and molders through millennia. I call this phenomenon the liberal culture—as it uses cultural means for its expansion, and exploits liberalism's hard-won principles of social and political interplay. The circumstance that liberalism is unable to rid itself of the liberal culture's companionship somehow attests to its decline.

Ideologically, the culture of the last decades has leaned toward the world-view that sees progress in unburdening man from bonds proposed to him by reason and civilization, and in assuring him of the overrriding importance of his individual instincts and propensities. In the 1960's, that trend began to swell with blatant deviations of idea and behavior, which became commonly known as the counter-culture. This was an ominous misnomer, as if one had made a religious token out of a Beatles' album cover. There have been a few counter-cultures in history, all of them founded on replacing deeply entrenched values and views with diametrically opposite ones. When the Jews announced to the polytheistic world that there was only one God—this was counterculture. When Christ proclaimed love as the ultimate value to Jews, whose ultimate value was obedience to Yahweh, and to Romans, whose supreme norm was civic law—this was counterculture. The Renaissance was counterculture, so was the Enlightenment, and even Marxism. But what was propagandized, pushed, publicized and championed at the end of the 60's in America was the emergence of a sleazy subculture, blown out of proportion by its commercial marketing as a novelty, and based on the misuse of the word "liberation." Liberating a society from reason and civility is a contradiction in terms—but this was the sole deliverance this subculture had to offer. The subculture movement survived by operating upon a false and foolish pretense that a motley of private mishaps, expressed with the help of pop music and journalism, was a common social condition. It lived by disdaining old wisdoms and adulating old hairdos, clothes and imagery. It sanctified that strange quirk in the liberal mind that considers Indian, black or Puerto Rican faithfulness to the past and to tradition a treasure, an old *cultural* value; in contrast, it scorned any beauty found in American patriotism, Christian traditions or Jewish orthodoxy—calling them corny, icky, reactionary, inhuman, repulsive and vulgar.

Whenever a true counterculture has emerged and put up a fight for its values, monuments of thought and art have marked its arrival and challenge; things are never the same afterwards. The subculture of the 60's proved to be dolefully noncreative. Nothing of genuineness and importance in thought, letters or the arts appeared during its ten-year presence in the mainstream of the American culture. It succeeded only in superimposing an interest in runty people whose claims to be in the news, literature and movies were their hang-ups, breakdowns, psychic and anatomical deformations and seediness. It has never been explained why we should have been involved with the tawdry dillemas of dwarfs who made it in advertising, cheap music and TV sit-coms, and who lacked nothing except common sense and moral fiber. Why the virtues and intelligence which were assailed by doubts and adversities had to be banned from fiction writing. Why *this* culture, contaminated by a subculture, insisted that crass morons and rascals from its plays and films motivated by irrationality and meanness, should be considered as wronged by society and not by themselves, has never been convincingly explained. Why they deserved our compassion, respect and recognition, while we and our children were supposed to emulate their phony, shallow unhappiness, remained a secret.

The liberal culture has a philosophy. It is based on mistaking the spontaneity of life instincts for indeterminism. Such a view of the nature of life brings license forward as the ultimate guide for existence and behavior—it establishes the "truth" that whatever is permitted is right and good, and whatever prohibited wrong and bad. The ontology and humanism that derive from such a vision must inevitably lead to what D. H. Lawrence described as "the village-idiot mind, playing with muck."

The liberal culture has its surrogate of religion. It centers on the cult of incoherence of thought and instincts, constantly advertised through the cultural media as a salutary and propitious alternative to codified and organized human endeavors. Such religiosity was once perceived as eccentricity and inanity; today, its libcultural version has a tremendous capability to mess up human lives.

The liberal culture has its ethics. It deems indulgence superior to love. It advocates normlessness of emotions and persecutes any preference for moral order. It promotes amorphous latitude in lieu of a principled commitment to passion or person.

The liberal culture has its psychology, or, in point of fact, favors the wholesale substitution of psychology for religious and lay morality. Libcultural psychology is supposed to be the answer to all existential enigmas, and the supreme guiding agent of soul and mind. It has resulted in the daily newspapers championing an adaptability to neuroses as a triumph of progress and social conscience. If we feel lower than Sodomites in the area of mores these days, it is because the libcultural psychology has established every animalism and bestiality of impulse and predisposition as acceptable or tolerable. The Sodomites, to their advantage, didn't have cameras and fast-printing presses, which the liberal culture monopolizes. The foremost casualty of the libculture fascination with psychology is the human sense of normalcy which is being wiped out of our current reality. The most helpless prey: children who are being robbed of their childhood by rampant pornography, libcultural psychology's favorite toy. Libcultural psychology operates virtually unopposed by the social forces that traditionally influence consciousness and behavior. To the contrary, one has the impression that a monstrous collusion of cultural influences—from the *New York Times* to *Newsweek* to *Vogue* to the liberal faculties of Ivy League universities—is trying its best to implant libcultural psychology's supposition that self-destruction is the primary privilege of an individual and a society. An atmosphere of murderous laxity in which *everything* can be inflicted on *everybody* for a cheap price is created daily by the media. Sexual molestation of children is nothing new, however, it has never been a cultural prerogative endorsed by psychology. It is now.

The liberal culture has its own sociology. It peddles the shapelessness of social interaction as freedom, and anarchic egomania as egalitarianism. It mercilessly extirpates common sense from politics and economics. It superimposes ideological divisiveness upon the American family and politicizes both the dinner table and the movie house. It fanatically touts the legislation and bureaucratization of moral and personal sensitivities. Feelings are forcibly kneaded by libcultural sociology into platitudes determining our social conduct and private destinies. Feminism, the libculture's perversion of the educational process, half-baked theories of crime, justice, and the penitentiary system leading contributors to the decay of the American civilization.

And, of course, liberal culture has its aesthetics, literature, arts, and its overpowering cultural credo. Its creativity of this vein has brought us to the point where the distinction between brutal explicitness and sincerity has been lost. The abominable has been declared beautiful and equated with innocence. The liberal culture has entered a claim that the degenerate be given not only equal rights and compassion, but also a title to artistry—and he has gotten it all. It has declared the responsibility for vice null, thus opening the door to miserable sophists who extort fame and honors that society once reserved for prophets. Liberationism—that weird progeny of the liberal culture—has come to mean both ideology and way of life: it has made people claim that they should be freed from the prerequisites of civilization, marriage, driving regulations and breakfast habits. Needless-to-say, such an "ideology" is less amusing when it causes acts of imbecility, reduces people to doleful marionettes, and wreaks havoc in human lives. The most ominous feature of the liberal culture—its mortal sin—is the cultivation of moods of disintegration and decomposition. These have been translated into pop-cultural fare by countless books, movies, plays, rock concerts—while the liberal critics and teachers declare them humanity's deliverance. The libculture's sway over the media and entertainment industry has endowed the psychopath, the deviate, the vicious criminal humanoid with the status of cultural hero. As E. W. F. Tomlin puts it in his excellent essay ("Intellectual Treason," in the British *New Universities Quarterly,* Summer 1978):

"Low and deviant tastes have been catered for in every society, but never before have they been deliberately moulded."

*

"A climate of legalized lie and hypocrisy, which pervades a substantial sphere of the American reality, differs very little from the Soviet cant. There—it is an official cant imposed by the party and state bureaucracy, here—cant is manipulated into social rules by the liberal intellectual elite. In other words: their lie is totalitarian, ours democratic..."

This is an opinion of a keen Polish observer of both contemporary scenes. The American intellectual elite, with the exception of a disproportionate minority, is in the bondage of the liberal culture.

Thus, we have a curious paradox. Throughout our history, commoners have lived within a framework of the official culture, while elites, or social fringes, created their own, often antithetic subcultures. They were called schismatic, nonconformist, Bohemian. The liberal culture, with its outlawing of normalcy and cancellation of common sense, fits perfectly into the rebellion of the periphery. However, things have become hopelessly mixed up. On the one hand, liberal culture has all-encompassing ambitions to become the official culture. It is not far from reaching this goal when little old ladies from Dubuque are the eager buyers of *Hustler* in motel newsstands far from home; and all a beefy Midwestern farmer hopes for is to look like Rod Stewart at his Sunday barn disco. On the other hand, the honor of rebelling has been passed to the common people. When the PTA combats the libcultural TV degeneracy, it's the society which has become independent and nonconformist, whereas the intellectual elites and self-styled outcasts cringe and bootlick the libcultural officialdom. Unfortunately for them, and regardless of their burning desire to be iconoclasts and firebrands, nowadays they are in fact the incarnation of a despicable establishment. A liberal-cultural one.

CHAPTER 4

The Ugly
Beautiful People*

In our day, the ugly beautiful people have become an ideological occurrence. When the governor of California semiofficially travels abroad with sexual service personnel in lieu of a spouse, this is not non-conformism but an ideological statement. It is calculated to attract favor from trendsetters whom he deems more important than ordinary constituents. A very private aide to a governor is nothing new. Intense publicity for less traditional proclivities of a politician is new. It takes into account that America is divided into two cultures, each living by its own principles and styles. But only one is hailed by the monopolistic liberal media as progressive and wholesome—the normless and amorphous ethos of the Manhattan-Malibu axis. And some governors are banking on its electoral power.

Every society has an effluvium, but effluvia, even the most noxious ones, rarely become ethical problems. They have in today's America. The *lumpen* is now called an underclass, seen as a source of morality; the *canaille* has gone through a beautification process and now has its saints, like Genet, and pious apologists, like film director Robert Altman. The ugly beautiful people, the American effluvium, once even aimed at becoming an elite, but the sheer force of numbers (a result of American affluence) has expanded them into another underclass.

Historically, elites have always been formed through a concentration of either political or financial power that rarefied itself into a social standing; attempts to form elites on the basis of moral or civic virtues, sadly, have seldom succeeded. However, in the past, elites as a rule tried to work out a virtuous image: the aristocratic ethics of honor and protectiveness, or the bourgeois morality of industriousness and economic plenty were socially functional. Rectitude was always a vital factor in their ideologies, even if it had to be propounded at the price of hypocrisy. The lower classes—for whom love, family and personal honesty were accessible values—had the official aristocratic propaganda of decorum and the bourgeois propaganda of decency for supports in gathering the existential assets of life, work, traditions. Providing well-defined values, even if they were not always implemented in practice, accounted for the health and success of Western civilization. It determined its universal mission.

Today, the ugly beautiful people's pretense of an elite results from the fusion of technology and culture. Deprived of philosophy and faith, they use cultural bric-a-brac—lifestyles, fashion, pop art—as their spiritual identification and dialectics. With their moral stimuli in a condition of atrophy, they couldn't survive without the support of the press, electronic communications, movies, TV. In fact, their only recognizable tenet: "Fun *Is* Morality," repulsive as it is, serves as fuel for the sensationalist media.

Their social bases are non productive professions that enrich neither society nor culture, only decorate them. Each civilization in history had its milieu of drones, parasites and spongers, whose group rationale was the "embellishment" of drab reality. In the past, those groups elicited little more than amused contempt from their contemporaries. In today's America, this "embellishment" has become an irrationally respected and absurdly lucrative profession. This makes the ugly beautiful people thirsty for outright social power, which they actually are close to attaining through various interactions with and feedbacks from authentic elites.

Every profession contributes something to the overall performance of a highly specialized economy. However, the production of entertainment, false eyelashes and neckties is not of the same contributory import as bread, coal and light bulbs. A free market economy is supposed to pay for what's in demand. Yet, at some point, generating an artificial demand for shoddiness and trash, and pushing up financial rewards for utterly reprehensible services, became the mainstays of nonproductive professions. The overpayment for effluvial "embellishment" is slowly emerging as the grave mistake of our civilization. A mood has been created, no doubt detrimental to our interests as a whole, in which a fashion designer or rock impresario is anomalously entitled to be better off than someone who produces knowledge or enlightened attitudes, or an educator who exerts himself to improve human conduct. This juxtaposition of facts is slowly turning into a social caricature. A successful entertainer is paid grotesquely more than a nurse, although the latter is infinitely more morally and socially worthy. In the ugly beautiful people's dialect this is explained by "talent" as a marketable value, but a talent to entertain in healthier societies was considered a private quality and usually dispensed for free. It's only been since technology began its woeful interaction with the production of culture that the bloodsucking careers of singing stars, literary agents, dope theorists, professional freaks, acting hacks, publicity stuntmen, have invaded the parasitic fringe of the vocational idlers, turned them into an underclass, and with the help of the corrupted media promoted the ugly beautiful folklore into an all-American exemplar. The "embellishment" rationalization has been expanded into a *Weltanschauung,* ugly, miscreated and foul as it is, but relentlessly promoted and—what's ominous— economically profitable. It subsists on psychoanalytical twaddle which makes platitudes into "wisdom" that legislates existences and emotions. It creates a pseudointellectual climate in which the pop-art mass magazine critics, the current spiritual leadership, anoint "greatness" and are paid out of all reasonable proportion to their social worth. Why perfunctory and embarrassingly shallow journalistic renditions of history, contemporary affairs, behavioral issues and artistic creativity time and again have become multimillion dollar enterprises is a crucial question. The answer probably is: Because the greedy and unscrupulous liberal publisher strikes an alliance with the liberal media manipulator, and together they set out to boost at any price a conformist liberal critic, or a liberal intellectual bigot, thereby forming the most formidable sociocultural device of our time. They all frequent the same leisure circuit; at their cocktail parties and carefully crafted cultural events, the gathering and inbreeding of mutual supportiveness is taking place. Next morning, it passes into publishing and editorial offices, or movie studios, and the warped liberal ideals get blended with journalistic hype and with a communication system that feeds and thrives on everything value-free, offbeat, far-out. Opinion making for the mere sake of opinion making has become a tremendous, all-encompassing industry.

In such a climate, inversion and perversion of meanings becomes both a basic instrument of "change" and a source of unholy profits. The acting profession, for one, though certainly an artistic skill, was never held in high esteem in refined civilizations: actors made their living by impersonating other people, somehow an offense to the Judeo-Christian sense of God-given human properties. Among the ugly beautiful people, actors equal ancient prophets. But not only has the actor's role been blown out of proportion, the entire mechanism of culture has been corrupted.

For over six decades, Hollywood mirrored the character and dreams of the nation. It did it in a garish way, and was called the cradle of a vibrant and folksy art. Simple-mindedness and tinsel, always Hollywood's image, did not prevent it from capturing some essential truths about America, which commanded the attention and sentiments of the world at large. During the '60s, Hollywood was put on another course, hailed as "creative" and "introspective" by liberal elites. Movies began to reflect the marginal rather than the essential, aberrations of reality rather than reality itself. Instead of dreams, we are offered nightmares which were declared self-questioning insights. To claim that *The Exorcist, Jaws* or *A Wedding* represent anything but the sleazy periphery of truth is not only a fraud, but also the main factor in Hollywood's degeneration to the repulsiveness of a jaded stripteaser whose only ambition is to shock and to make money. This fundamental change in creative trends has had many consequences: among them, some new ways have materialized for the celebrity elites to live, love and influence the cultural aura of the country.

The ugly beautifuls are on the uppermost end of the affluence scale, but their political orientation is intensely radical and leftish. This has something to do with the present marketability of leftism, radical chic, and other demonstrable cliches; it can be safely assumed that any political extremism of any totalitarian brand would be warmly embraced by them, provided its meretriciousness would supply maximum visibility. The owner of a prosperous Manhattan disco, who obviously culls his astronomic income from pimpish instincts, declared to awed reporters that he was "against Vietnam" and "would never go." The central ideological and theoretical organ of the ugly beautifuls, *Women's Wear Daily,* frantically promotes penthouse radicalism and overtly communist pop singers and "poets," goes into raptures at any modish cause, rally, etc. It also attempts to idealize its stance; normlessness and dissipation are presented in its pages as a fight against hypocrisy, constriction, convention. A fabulously rich film director unveils his proclivity to stealing and touts it as "moral" impulse: "I like robbers . . . they are some of the finest people I ever met," he crows, and *WWD* reports it with pride.

It has already become clear that, in spite of all liberal media efforts, there's an unbridgeable rift between the common people and the ugly beautiful people of America. In fact, the latter are the former's openly declared enemy. Two kinds of money earned by two kinds of people have obviously civilizational consequences: those who provide food, electricity and transportation are pitched against the producers of news, entertainment, pop art and distorted liberal ideas. The ugly beautiful people are the focus of contention: the first loathe them, the second not only tolerate them but permit them to act as their legitimate elite. The first still think that patriotism and the Boy Scouts are good things; the second reject anticommunism, falsely present themselves as underdogs fighting on the side of other underdogs from their Beverly Hills mansions, and serve cocaine at their parties in the name of sacred solidarity with the oppressed. Being recklessly pushed by the media as the paradigm of American success, these ugly, mean, cynical, most often brainless people, who made it into the spotlight, ultimately ruin the common man's social chance to live better. As the alliance between the ugly beautifuls and the peddlers of liberal culture perennially needs an enemy on whom it can prey and structure its power of vilification, the producer of energy and housing becomes its natural victim. He is unable to create a fasionable cultural image; deprived of cultural weapons, his defenselessness becomes an easy source of money and fame for the liberal ugly beautiful predator. His intentions are smartly defamed, his preferences become the new American demonology. Cultural con men lavishly live off his denunciation. He has little social power and only some vestiges of political power. (Nothing exemplifies this better than the "memoirs" of Margaret Trudeau; when we realize that her lover during her marriage to the prime minister of Canada was the owner of Club Mediterranee, the largest bordello empire on earth, some new, intertwined political potentialities become obvious.)

In the end, it's all a strange, if not tragic, contradiction of democratic capitalism. Why, at its most advanced stage, does it still remunerate with money work, thrift, enterprise, innovation, reliability and courage in economic life, while, at the same time, lavishly granting fame and millionaire wealth to vulgarity, destruction, sham, wickedness, lies, expediency, obsequiousness to fads, stupidity, meanness, bestiality in culture? In short—why does it reward the ugly beautiful people with exorbitant success? It was not always thus; as it stands now, capitalism is, in the long run, the loser, in spite of some instant bonanzas for the record companies and TV corporations. With the help of a perverted First Amendment, which was not conceived as a privilege, but as a principle of mutual obligation, an insidiously mighty group exploits a bogus populistic rhetoric in order to accrue immense wealth and use it to corrupt the American culture. The only real title to populism is the sharing of people's historic condition and needs. Nothing is further from that than the multibillion dollar entertainment industries run by the ugly beautiful people who frauduently claim solidarity with the American people. Since the liberal culture that backs them is by now a dogmatic orthodoxy, anyone who opposes them must be branded as reactionary, redneck, low-brow, yahoo, etc. Which, in turn, makes a merciless struggle inevitable.

CHAPTER 5

The Sin Of Incoherence*

Liberals are not a political party but they have a party line. This makes them an ideological faction. They are committed to the freedom of imposing their righteousness on everyone, regardless of individual preference or consent. They claim the privilege of dictating what's good to others in the name of what they have decided is good. The main source of their judgments is not reason or experience, but conscience—a blind impulse that tells them good from bad and right from wrong. "Liberty of conscience is the first step to having a religion—" William Penn wrote prophetically in 1673. And correctly so—as the 18th century protest of reason against religion, liberals' earliest preoccupation in history, has now become for them a matter of conscience; that is, a righteousness rooted in emotions and inclinations which justify any departure from coherence and rationality. In keeping with Penn's clairvoyance, the pages of the most distinguished dispensers of modern liberalism—*The New York Times, Washington Post, Time, The New Yorker, The New York Review of Books*—attest to the practice of turning liberalism into a religious dogma through their refusal to acknowledge adverse views through a fair discourse. There follows an unspoken tenet that the distribution of truths and values in America must be regulated solely by the liberal monopoly in response to every existential dilemma or social ill.

Thus, for instance, if people somewhere vote to ban smut from their community, the liberals fight fiercely for the freedom of smut peddlers to do their thing there; the fact that it means forcing pornography upon those who reject it, the liberals dismiss as immaterial. They deem themselves defenders of the morality of freedom, and coercing people to accept what they do not want is seen by the liberals as enlarging the moral horizons and enriching the sensibilities of the unenlightened. Culture structured on such a premise proves to be strangely disjointed and conformist in the same breath. The communicants of this faith tend to discount coherent social and moral criteria, but they herd together and collectively cringe before every fashion and fad which comes from any authority anointed by the liberal canon. Accountability is rejected as a norm in all areas of life.

The war and political scandals of the Sixties and Seventies will probably fade into history much sooner than the sociomoral incoherence that has risen to ascendance in the same period, and which Daniel Bell aptly has called "the postindustrial irrationalism." The prior decade saw children of opulent suburbia being pampered to the point of grotesqueness by their free-wheeling, well-to-do parents. They acquired a preordained ignorance at the best universities from faculties whose prevailing segment dreamed of political power via a Marxism tailored to their swanky poses. People of wealth developed a decadent craving for abomination, clownish freakishness and fake indigence, all of which were supposed to express the nightmare of existence, one difficult to find in reality. These "kids" then converted splashy callousness and syrupy social sentimentality of modish attitudes into their own "new morality," to which the media responded with an ecstatic rapture. They began to throw bombs for the sake of a "people's revolution" that real people, poor as well as rich, loathed, feared and scorned.* For the sin of rejecting them, the enormous majority of American citizens, who still respected traditional ideals, was declared despicable by the "enlightened" strata. Still, common folks were not immune to the itch of incoherence: the big city unions went overboard pursuing a $20,000 wage for garbage men, ignoring the fact that there's an objective economic difference between sanitation and plasma physics in their services to a society. Furthermore, a sweeping number of serene people, swearing that their only goal in life was honest work, an effort to harvest a crop and to supply people with it, hatefully rejected capitalism, the sole economic system that coherently fuses hard work and a large harvest, and joined communes where they spent years taking drugs, discussing production and producing illegitimate children but scarcely the means to provide for them. During the same period, people, who could say and do whatever they wished, publicly screamed through gigantic amplifiers that they felt suppressed and enslaved, and staged monstrous demonstrations to impose by decibel their feelings on all those who doubted the truth of their assertions. Highly-paid columnists extolled in windy articles the validity of those who demanded freedom in America, mysteriously failing to note that the blusterers had never been restrained from anything by anybody. And soon homosexuals demanded that they be included within the definition of normalcy.

Some now say: those were the throes of transition from one America to another, which have now passed and formed the foundation for a new American tradition. But have the throes passed away, and is the new pattern visible?

Both the Jeffersonian ideal of agricultural economics and rural culture, and the subsequent industrial age of aggressive management and skilled labor, created sociocultural climates in America. Mammoth cities with multiplying social problems still sustained a coherence of human exertions, goals and means. Some believe that the attack on congruity began with the burgeoning of suburbia which has become a psychological desert, a breeding ground for

---

*During the Columbia University rebellion in 1968, a student had been complaining before the TV cameras that it was impossible to make revolution in America because the "people are too happy." A decade later, a "child of the '60s" bitterly echoed him in the radical *Village Voice*, deploring that revolution was impossible because there were no hungry people in America. She, of course, would have preferred widespread starvation to make revolution possible.

neuroses, an American Kabuki theater of gestures and attitudes expressing the unimportance of logic in performing the rites of affluence. Culminating in the '60s, the liberal culture was obviously the child of a love affair between plush suburbia and the American academe infested with arrogant and hedonistic leftism. It was an alliance powerful enough to shatter the tradition that prosperity imposes duties and responsibilities for cultural elevation and civic betterment, a tradition which earlier had produced in America a vital and creative culture. Now, in our days, we still witness the stubborn legacy of disjointedness as a mode of thinking and a behavorial ideal. The liberal culture has two ridiculously discrepant standards for its endorsement of sexual incontinence. Reviewing a movie entitled *Madam Kitty*, which depicts Nazi Germany's orgiastic scene, the liberal critics described the latter as "depraved, decadent, damned"; but liberal culture's New York lighthouse, the Village Voice, calls a parlor house that sports the frolicsome name of Plato's Retreat and specializes in collective fornication, a "group-sex pleasure-dome." On a Manhattan street some of the unwashed creatures in the filthy garb of a Bolshevik commissar, a Red-Chinese party agitator, or a Cuban guerilla, turn out to be millionaires, lawyers, admen, gynecologists or psychoanalysts who have paid Bloomingdale's a fortune to look "stylish." Why this mix of financial success with behavioral imbecility? The liberal culture's adherents are leftish for they are infantile in their demeanor, or infantile because they worship zany leftism—and the identification of childishness with an excessive left zealotry is not my diagnosis but Lenin's.

The demolition of the sense of one's obligation toward society, or to another person, or even to one's self, is best shown in the liberal culture's most incoherent demand for unqualified acceptance of everybody by everybody. According to the liberal culture's gospel, humanness should manifest itself in "sympathy" and "compassion" of everyone for everyone, even for those with animalistic propensities, even for Mick Jagger, even for Reverend Jim Jones, even for Jack Abbott. This silly attitude is not rooted in Christian good will, but in the "in" pseudofriendship for *others*, in spurious fellowship that assumes "grooviness" in every random interhuman relationship. Certainly, an allegiance to such a "commandment" must be constantly faked, as feeling solidarity with everyone is not human but a doctrinal postulate, and it presumes the elimination of the genuine human apparatus of choice, preference, selection. To my mind, no sane individual could profess solidarity with the Plasmatics rock group, Jane Fonda or Andy Warhol—all demisaints of the liberal culture. But the unconditional acceptance of the other is the supreme libculture virtue, a mighty agent of reigning incoherence, and it is daily imposed upon us by the cultural climate manufactured by the liberal media and entertainment industry.

An American today is supposed to live according to musts designated by the liberal culture: he must accept rock music because it allegedly expressed the torment of the youth and a quest for a better world; he must accept frontal nudity as proof of artistic sincerity (which improves the quality of our lives); he must refrain from seeking retribution when urban looters go on a rampage because such dimwitted passivity is thought to be rewarded sometimes with a restructured and better society. Books and movies tell him to express sympathy and understanding even when his woman is raped by a junkie, for this kind of magnanimity is currently considered the higher stage of humanness; he is expected to feel affinity with a physically repulsive performer of punk rock who is endowed with the mentality of a rat, because according to the liberals who govern culture, this disgusting singer is a homo sapiens and our future in one. The looter and the punk are *the others* who must be reformed through our sympathy, understanding, even love. Therefore, they have a right to encroach upon us, live off our taxes, invade our lives in every possible way—be it as newsmaking objects of Time magazine's and CBS News' loving attention, or just as newsworthy criminals who should be rehabilitated but not punished. In tune with the liberal culture's evangelism, they are unaccountable for any of their aggressive protests against the "unresponsive, heartless" society.

Our natural moral and physical revulsion is, of course, termed inhumanity, misanthropy, bigotry, although for centuries, a response of disgust in such circumstances has been recognized as a sign of civilized maturity. Refusing to accept the liberals' cheap cliches, their shallow social moralizing, we are called names. Pointing out that we, the victims of these modern barbarities, also have moral sensitivities, we are branded as antihuman and antisocial. If we ask that *the others*—the deranged film stars, exhibitionists, youth gangs, deviates and "progressive" tycoons of pornography—acknowledge an obligation to consider our concept of propriety, we receive the ultimate insult, the label of reactionaries. And neither politics nor law gives us any recourse, as our detractors control culture, the all-pervading element which makes the American people their helpless victim. *Their* culture gives them the opportunity to preach freedom and humanity endlessly and practice an all-out assault on minds and principles.

Once one fully recognizes the link between incoherence and the liberal culture, he perceives innumerable examples of this interaction in education, welfare programs, psychology, foreign policy and almost any field he considers. The suicidal effort to destroy the law-enforcement agencies can then be explained. Here is the root cause of high school illiteracy and the narrowmindedness of so many college graduates. It becomes blatantly visible how the liberal culture works against the very instincts of the society, how the public yearning for stability and order is constantly disrupted by the artificially stimulated trepidations to "alert" the public's conscience. Someone remarked not long ago that what has happened to America is mirrored in the difference between the two New York blackouts: the 1965 one was characterized by civic attitudes that could be described as manifestations of human solidarity; the 1977 one spelled anarchy. The time span between them marks the total domination of the liberal culture, which during this period relentlessly imposed on us the principle that moral responsibility equals civil death.

What can be done to confront the liberal culture and expose its sin of incoherence?

We must organize cultural and educational arsenals of ideas to detect and identify perniciousness. We must encourage in the society a lively distrust of the liberal culture and a rejection of incoherence, and convince Americans that only prudence and caution in accepting that culture's offerings can open the door to an affirmative renewal of the salutary traditions of Western civilization. We have enough intellectual resources to undertake such a task. In contrast to the liberal culture's ethics, we want not to impose our ideas on others, but to argue for them publicly, confident of their success if rationality and logic are given a chance. We must refuse to support those universities, publications, movie companies and publishing houses, which spurn such a dialogue, which cast aside our argumentation without a hearing.

By the end of the 1970's, in a letter to *Time* magazine (that pillar of the liberal culture), a woman wrote:

"... When I look at this country, a modern-day Babylon that is fast approaching its twilight, and see it wallowing in decadence, corruption, immorality and banality, I am proud to realize that absolutely none of it is of my making."

I understand the lady's anguish, but do not share her pessimism. I, for one, see no twilight around us yet. I believe America still is graced with enough decent people and enough robust institutions so that it does not fit into the simplistic "modern-day Babylon" simile. And though, to my knowledge, I did nothing to contribute to the liberal culture and its incoherence, I feel some responsibility for its "making." For I see it as my duty to identify the harm created by immorality, error, insensitivity, muddle, imbecility, narrowmindedness, bigotry, cynicism and perversion, and to do my best to dispel their poisonous fumes. Even though I am conscious that such an effort may never end.

CHAPTER 6

The Cult of Deficient Thinking*

I see the liberal culture as resting on many mighty pillars, one of the most powerful of which is the cult of deficient thinking.

The symptoms of the latter are everywhere. Its effect is the erosion of the American ethos, that is of the set of principles and values by which this nation *wishes* to live. Even if America's efforts have fallen short now and then, in making this wish come true, this wish has always conditioned America's fortunes as an *ideal* worth striving for.

Its disintegration has many causes, of which the most disturbing is, perhaps, the perversion of freedom. Freedom is America's element, a sort of force of nature, with all the blessings and unpredictability of naturalness. An extremist approach to freedom, however, brings more harm than good: it is as if we imagined precipitation as not only a fertilizer of crops, but as something we are constitutionally forbidden to take shelter from. Freedom converted into licentiousness threatens the fabric of organized life; all we need is common sense to tell us this. In the '60s, freedom as an absolute brought us a specific moral vacuousness as a proclaimed beneficence. Many saw in it a breeding ground for "new" virtues. "New virtues?" Saul Bellow wondered in *To Jerusalem and Back*, "Are there any?" Neither theorists nor practitioners of the liberal culture could have answered his question. "New" virtues is a classic construct of deficient thinking. Integrity, truthfulness, independence of mind, loyalty, heroism are as old as mankind and nothing indicates their obsolescence.

The cult of deficient thinking is a complex phenomenon. Its ubiquity makes it unassailable. Neither formal knowledge, nor moral courage, nor even wisdom, is sufficient to expose it clearly and irrefutably. One of the few effective weapons against it is common sense—that is the human faculty to be adamant that 2 and 2 makes 4 not 5. This is why the liberal culture is hellbent on eradicating common sense from the face of the earth; it denigrates and villifies it at each step, and calls it the low-brow philosophy of rednecks.

Some areas of social actuality have gathered more of the cult's intoxicating dust than others. Until recently, man and woman shared both an existence and the human condition. The code of their interdependence has, through the millennia, been ratified by *both* nature and civilization. Recently, the code was declared invalid and replaced with a separateness of goals: the basic premise of modern feminism is that man and woman *can* exist without one another. The divorce of destinies is supposed to bring absolute parity, thus improvement of humanity.

*Editorial for *Chronicles of Culture* in the March/April issue 1978. (Vol. 2, No. 2)

Common sense whispers into our souls that this is deficient thinking; that, in the end, it will terminate the mutual *need* which man feels for woman, and vice versa. This need has always been the nonbiological DNA, the source of human life on this planet. Men and women have always known that it is difficult to live *with* one another and impossible *without*. It is a self-evident truth and its denial drowns us in grotesque abominations. However, countless books and movies promote the aberration daily in print and on the airwaves: they intensely advocate the abrogation of the sexes, while serious critics recommend their messages as a panacea for man's and woman's ills. A fallacy originating in fantasies has been molded into an almost compulsory belief and is being injected into minds. The deception is so gross, and its promoters are so shrill, that it can be categorized neither as faith, nor as idea—only as cult.

Under the liberal culture's sway, social morality has become a paradise of deficient thinking. After the demise of sin, accused of having been just a figment of religiosity, the ultimate relativization of guilt turned big cities into jungles—a metaphor unfair to the latter, for no one purposelessly takes life in a jungle. The cultists assume that a scientifically prescribed morality can legislate consciences, they worship the academic Baal on every TV talk show. In the light of this ethic, and according to its frequent social implementations, both Lady Macbeth and Raskolnikov, for example, would be unpunishable if their crimes were uncovered with the help of unauthorized bugging. More liberal courts may even deem Shakespeare's and Dostoyevski's literary imagination a fully inappropriate device to opine on what's guilt; in such a case we have to assume that both the Scottish lady and the Russian student would have been acquitted. And common sense tells us that there is something oddly deficient in this approach to morality and law.

In a recent story, *Time*—that stronghold of listless "objectivity"—reported on the unheard-of crimes that are being committed daily in American high schools, once the incubators of civic virtues. The magazine ascribed the anarchy of conduct and atrophy of humaneness to the downfall of authority in the '60s. But it does not mention that *ideas*—especially moral ones—brought about this collapse. Those were half-baked, meretricious concepts of liberation, right and wrong, individual conscience as the supreme guidance. They were promoted by specious "philosophers" and "moralists," who, in turn, were given frenetic advertisement in the pages of *Time*. It was cheap and easy to become a "spiritual leader" in those times; it sufficed to climb a soap box and shout: "War is Evil!" or: "People Are Beautiful!" or anything equally profound and revealing, to earn the cheers of spaced-out crowds, and the enthusiastic reports of the national magazines. The leaders and crowds vanished, but the sleazy ideas have stayed with us, and today they flourish in the nation's high schools, and give rise to the crudest violence a society in peace has ever known. Those who preached such ideas still call themselves liberals, or radicals, today, and are still venerated by *Time* for their never-ending quest for the perfectibility of man to be achieved through equating every possible wickedness and derangement with the common-sensical desire for normalcy and order. The result of their domination of culture is that vice and sin are among us to a degree unknown to previous generations. Many of them now have second thoughts, but they will still crucify anyone who would say that evil and decency cannot have an equal footing in a society that wants to survive and remain free. Common sense warns us that their thinking is deficient and leads to a disaster which may destroy us all, the cultists included.

In other fields of intellectual endeavor, the cult of deficient thinking rages with no less impunity. However monstrous and detailed the contrary evidence, the anti-American scholars, trained and paid by American universities, will incessantly come up with books proving that America is to be blamed for the Cold War. Some concede that the guilt is on both sides. Rash is the academic who would dare to admit that it is Russia, and Russia alone, who initiated it, wanted it and needed it for mostly domestic reasons, although that proof can be found in every primer for the use of Soviet children, and the written testimony of scholars whose literature on the subject could encircle the globe.

The anti-CIA paranoia, the paradigm of deficient thinking, performed and practiced by the foremost and best respected press organs in the country, turns on occasion into a parody of the primary rules of reasoning. Some cultists of deficient thinking, highly-rated as beacons of liberal conscience, publicly demand that law enforcement and intelligence agencies keep watching only people guilty of misdeeds and betrayals. How those agencies can know without surveillance who's guilty of nasty things and who's not, the cultists do not explain. Now, even a village fool knows that to detect hidden wrongdoing one must sniff it out. A spy is a spy because he tells nobody who he is—this simple truth has been confirmed by both semantics and experience, other comportment would indicate another profession. Intentional murderers are not ostentatious, because an openness could interfere with their intentions. However, the cultists do not notice that in Russia for any citizen to be bugged means an impending trip to a Gulag regardless of what was discovered by the procedure. While in America, Ms. Bella Abzug, once justly bugged because her ardors for Stalin kept proper authorities in suspense as to what she was *really* doing, has made a political career out of being bugged, rising to membership in Congress.

Now—here is a difference. The cultists of deficient thinking may not notice it, and this is why their mental processes seem defective. But common sense tells us that something in this situation is hopelessly twisted and falsified. After all, we have developed enough through centuries of civilization, culture and literature to perceive that Abel might have avoided death if he had had foreknowledge of Cain's designs. And that Abel's move to obtain such advance recognition by any means at his disposal would have appeared moral, proper and wise in the eyes of both God and man, for he was good and his heart was pure.

CHAPTER 7

Magazines and Unreason.*

The ambient incoherence of our reality is discounted by many as the classic illusion of changing times. The past always appears ordered, they say, the present chaotic. Astigmatic perspectives are certainly a fact of life, but I can remember times when things fell into congruity when someone honestly tried to arrange them. Epochs of all-encompassing incoherence are a part of history, but they do not constitute an organic element of existence.

The current wave of incoherence, I would tend to attribute to the preponderance of magazines. Their power seems underestimated, they are mostly perceived as a countless, blabbing family related to two boorish giants—the daily press and TV. Whether or not the giants listen to them—and they do indeed—the synergic impact of news-opinion-leisure and popcultural magazines on the popular mind is tremendous. They shape the reading American's *Weltanschauung,* his ideology, existential patterns, behavorial preferences, morality and eschatology, they instruct on how to live and how to die. They are America's Oxfords and Sorbonnes in Manhattan cubicles with braless receptionists, they concoct epistemology for mass-retailing. A crushing majority of Americans has learned the word *ethics* not from Plato, but from *Time* magazine. Each week or month they feature a locust swarm of Sophocleses in double-knit leisure suits to tell Americans about fate and inevitability, Balzacs and Conrads in Gucci loafers to inform them about society and duty, blue-denim Dostoyevskis and Freuds to elaborate on the murkiness of human souls, and cloned mini-Lenins in jogging gear to fast talk on social justice. Today America knows about democracy, misery, choice, pain, love, knowledge, failure, success, genitals, value, humanness, reason, procreation, sorrow, sacrifice and pointlessness from the magazines which are hell-bent on explaining it all.

The realm of the magazine is a large and shallow puddle in which the reflection of a rainbow is perfectly possible. For 30 years it has been the libcultural rainbow, a glossy source of incoherence, whose colors are not arranged according to the natural pattern but disarrayed by the liberal orientation which fills the puddle. If I had to enumerate what the liberal culture targets as its most insidious and implacable enemies in today's America, I would say: normalcy and common sense. It is mainly those elements of humanity which are injured in American magazines on a weekly or monthly basis. Add to this the magazines' cult of transiency and vogue—and we have the gloomy explication of why the ERA is rejected by women, taxpayers must

pay money to the bureaucrats who effect their rapid impoverishment, plutoc-
racy is supporting communist preachers, anarchy is called equality, neuroses
are hailed as progress. We seem to exist in a gigantic Helzapoppin on a
national scale, in which frantic amusement bubbles here and there, though, at
second glance, the hilarity suddenly evaporates. *Women's Wear Daily,* one of
the best informed specialty mouthpieces of the liberal culture, reported with
relish on Mr. Warren Burger's worries on a book about the courts Messrs.
Woodward and Armstrong welded together:

> "They've been going around the court saying they have all these
> secret documents, and trying to blackmail people into giving them
> information,' said Burger. 'The problem is, they're never willing to
> show anyone the documents. Their tactics are a lot like the ones
> Joe McCarthy used."

Considering that Mr. Burger is the U.S. Supreme Court Chief Justice, while
Messrs. Woodward and Armstrong are acknowledged highwaymen of American journalism, we can envisage this country drowning in a puddle—as comic
as it may sound.

It has become obvious that in this America, overrun by the liberal culture, a
new concept of un-American activities is slowly taking shape. The un-
American position seems to be that which fails to divorce freedom from
responsibility and humanism from good sense. And that which does not see
investigative journalism, in its libcultural version, as daredevil bravery and
intellectual nonconformity. Its victims, inept government or overregulated
business, are doleful underdogs these days: the myth of their formidability is
preserved artificially, as is the myth of the righteous purity of the investiga-
tors. Once upon a time, un-American activities were those which aimed at the
destruction of American values. Misunderstandings and excessive zealotry
marred the fight against them: after all, a belief in Marxism was not an
un-American activity. But spying for a Marxist state was, and is today. Today,
dismantling America at home and abroad seems to be a virtuous American
activity, opposing it un-American. The libcult insists on sentencing spies
according to the importance of the stolen intelligence; if their booty is less
significant, let them go free until they export the whole defense system to Cuba
or Vietnam. Then we'll punish them by casting at them reproachful glances
from the Gulags in Kolyma.

There is a liberal dogma which states that the liberal version of freedom,
justice, conscience, progress, pluralism is the only *American* concept of these
values, and the liberal press pounds it into minds with a ruthless ferocity. In
the liberal press there is a code sentence that says that the ERA is an
amendment designed to "outlaw discrimination on the basis of sex." No one
ever mentions that there is a giant shelf of congressional and state laws that
outlaws discrimination on the basis of sex, not to mention an entire library of
interpretative regulations daily enforced in every nook and cranny of the
American actuality.

Is this a matter of intellectual and ethical fairness? Far from it. And this unfairness is at the heart of the liberal concept of American pluralism. America is now more than ever a pluralistic society. But a dangerous myth has been deceptively sustained that the American culture is still open to the diversity of philosophical and ideological propositions, and that they all have an equal chance of being argued for and listened to. In point of fact, the more society, honoring its initial promise of equal human rights and opportunities, opens up to various ethnic groups, their traditions and folkloric paraphernalia, the more pluralism is expelled from the high culture. American culture, once the haven of free consciences and religious variety, has become monopolized by one ideological formation—"enlightened" and "progressive" liberalism.

Liberalism's perennial merit is that it early and forcefully endorsed human rights and privileges, and was ready to pick any fight in their defense. However, at some point, it confused the necessities of moral order grounded in reason, and opted for social order structured on speculative theories.

Professor Irving Howe, a distinguished liberal but by no means a libcultist, who is not shy to call himself a social-democrat, wrote not long ago that the foundation of American liberalism is reason. To my mind, the foundation of American liberalism, at least over the last 30 years of its dizzying career, is the blatant abuse of reason. It fought for a welfare state as the *economic* solution to the ills of a *capitalistic* economy. It propagated Big Government as the defender of freedoms and civil rights—a rather unreasonable supposition. In foreign policy, since World War II, liberalism has informed America that it has no right, and even less moral title, to tell the rest of the world how it should behave; until a few years ago, every staunch liberal insistingly demanded an attitude of reverence toward Russia—toward the same Russia that emerged from the last war as the only imperialistic power, enslaving free nations and enlarging its territory at others' expense. At the same time, the West began to disassemble colonialism under America's pressure. Every objection to unconditional love for Russia has been branded by American liberalism as Cold War tactics and American leaders of all stripes were burdened with the blame. Even now this is taking place as Russia begins to colonize Africa. If this is proof of the liberal obedience to reason, we may be losing a crucial tool which, since man's dawn, has warranted his very existence.

The *Chicago Tribune,* a chameleon of a newspaper, flannel-grey on its editorial pages, and liberal-pinkish in its cultural sections, not long ago ran another of its advertisements for procommunist books in the form of a review. The *Chicago Tribune* reviewer stated that the clear-cut anticommunism of the '40s and '50s was sinful, calamitous, repulsive, and, basically, an assault on innocent people and socially valuable organizations. It thus represented an ugly treason of American humanism and pluralism. The review was entitled: "A Painful Record that Illuminates a Dark Age." Why an epoch that brought America social stability, economic prosperity, flourishing of arts and crafts, and all-out progress in social mores, all of which became the entire planet's envy, can be called a "dark age" remains a mystery. Why the galactic American civilization should be characterized solely by its vigorous rejection of communism is another puzzle. The *Chicago Tribune's* review says that "the period was characterized by, above all, a suspension of due process of law," but does not mention the Rosenberg trial, considered even by America's foes a model of judiciary propriety unattainable even by the oldest European democracies. "Was there a viable Communist Party in America during the '30s and '40s? Did it present a legitimate threat to U.S. security?" asks the *Chicago Tribune* reviewer.

Well, I am from Eastern Europe. Whenever I read about the tribulations of Mr. Hiss and his adversaries, who still do not believe what he has been repeating for 30 years, I find them peculiarly irrelevant. If he lied, or passed state secrets, which it seems he did, it is not very nice, and he should have been punished for it. But what matters to me is the fact that, according to quite reliable Polish intelligence sources in London (during six years of war, it saved the allied command a lot of trouble), Mr. Hiss had telephone extension No. 3 within the American delegation at Yalta. No. 1 was Roosevelt, No. 2 was Harry Hopkins, Mr. Hiss instructed them both in how to negotiate with Stalin.

All the Soviet objectives for the post-war global order were attained at Yalta. Entire populations were slaughtered in Gulags. Old nations with flourishing cultures went into slavery. This is why Mr. Alger Hiss, in keeping with my sense of reason and conscience, deserves a life term, if not more.

CHAPTER 6

Toying With the Cultural Messages*

In the Middle Ages, an innocent-looking sixteen-year-old girl who had killed people at random would have been considered possessed by Satan, duly exorcised, and burned at the stake. A hundred years ago, she would have been seen as a victim of economic exploitation. Quite recently, social alienation, psychotic puberty, or improper relations with her father, would be the acceptable explanation. Now, it looks as if cultural moods and trends which affect Western civilization and are generated by ideas, may be the culprit.

Here is how it works.

From the morning radio news one learns that a middle-aged woman, upset by marital misfortunes, has hijacked a passenger jet with 131 persons aboard, and subjected them to the ordeals of terrorism — the bubonic plague of our age. The same broadcast informs us that a professional association of film critics has voted *Midnight Express* the year's best movie. Are these events correlated? Of course they are.

A couple of days later, 16-year-old Brenda Spencer opens fire on a crowded schoolyard in San Diego, kills two and wounds nine. Her motivation: "I just did it for the fun of it . . . I don't like Mondays." About the same time, one of the best-selling records in America is a new album of Ramones, a punk rock group; four scruffy idols of 16-year-olds sing: "I don't care 'bout poverty/ All I care 'bout is me . . ." Are these two facts interrelated? Of course they are.

Midnight Express is a movie glorifying heinous violence, pederasty and drug smuggling, all presented as human edification. *Time,* a journal of little compunction when it comes to freedom of the arts, called it "the ugliest sadomasochistic trip . . . that our thoroughly nasty movie age has produced." But Brenda could have seen it, it was not X-rated. In case she missed it, the *New York Times* "Special Features" serialized the book it was based on, and the *Chicago Tribune* ran it in installments. The idea that anyone should have access to bestiality in print and images may have libertarian merits, but it provides an open and massive support for mental and moral aberration on a social scale. When it is called value by academicians, jurists and the media, and defended with the help of the First Amendment, it unveils a socioethical abyss of scary dimensions. First and foremost, it creates a cultural climate that rapidly dissolves those obligations by which civilization lives and without which it cannot survive. Brenda Spencer exists amid the synergic pressures of the current pop-mass-cultural scene and soaks them up by natural osmosis. They are sanctified by fashion, by rewards, by their very omnipresence, and

by nothing. She lives her daily life with Kiss, another ignoble
g̶ ̶ ̶u̶p̶, a teenage ideological icon which proselytizes "Lust, Sweat and
Sex." At her age of 16, sex, whether she practices it or not, is for her a routinely
available commodity with disposable consequences, be it emotional or physical. All the time she sees its shoddiest symbolizations on TV and in tawdry
magazines on every newsstand, her teachers generally avoid the moral and
behavioral side of the issue, limiting themselves to hygienic technicalities. In
more serious outlets of culture, she finds a broadly accepted attitude that the
present state of sexual matters means progress, wholesome revolution against
prudery, a liberation of human mind and body. During the last 15 years, the
joint effort of psychologists, pornographers and the media has reduced sexuality and its manifestations to merely a physiological reaction, and Brenda's
is the first generation which has to live with this approach without an option
for how to embellish it with *other* fashions. She does not realize that sexual
activities were just function at mankind's dawn, and that the human race
imposed on itself countless conventions that were supposed to refine sexuality
into a source of values and emotions, and thereby enrich life. No one tells her
this; there's no cultural activity energized by fashionableness that could bring
to her *this* side of the story. The entire *Playboy-Hustler-Penthouse* syndrome,
with all the magnified and amplified hype of gloss and excitement, imposes on
Brenda the reverse. But there's no valid counteracting, no honest analysis, no
responsible critique by the interpretative organs of culture. No one, from
Newsweek to CBS to Paramount Pictures, makes her aware of, or visualizes
for her, the direct connection between cheapness of sex and that of human life;
and naturally, in our technotronic-mass-cultural setup, what's uncondemned
is mercilessly promoted. Stamping out the moral/emotional dimension of
sexuality creates a baneful vacuum in individual lives—and Brenda's "fun" is
directly related to it.

Those private demons that drive common humans, are still, sociology and
psychoanalysis notwithstanding, the most powerful elements of existence.
Religions and social ideas always related to them. But probably never before
were they more the products of a manipulative culture that has been transformed into an industry. The reasonable liberal looks with dread upon this
corruption conceived in his name: he sees how programmatic moral irresponsibility becomes the device of manipulators and he himself becomes prey of
the cultural nihilists who populate Manhattan publishing houses, the editorial
cubicles of the Chicago press and the Hollywood studios. Most of them
consider themselves "children of the '60s;" they still elevate petty frustrations
to the rank of moral dilemmas, and reduce conscience to the role of an
emotional dildo for superficial satisfactions. Hijacking planes, murder, arson,
drug peddling, blinding horses, raping boys, copulating in school corridors —
all this becomes material for "objective," "cool," "impartial" presentations,
and is often hailed as existential fulfillment. Massacres duly follow, either in
Guyana or in the lobbies of movie houses that offer *The Warriors*. There is no

one in this most variegated, richest and freest culture to convincingly tell Brenda Spencer "Thou shalt not kill . . . ," and, considering her life's cultural context, she could rightly view such a suggestion as a lack of consistency. She is the end product of a culture that has made a moral void a value, and triviality of death a natural law.

In Brenda, the old intellectual tradition of Western humanism, grounded in religion and philosophy, has come to its terminal perversion. Hitler's Germany and Stalin's Russia were only ominous station stops on this downward road. In America of the '70s, every daily paper brings evidence that neither medieval demonology, nor the 19th century positivist sociology, nor current psychological research, have explicative answers to the modern version of evil. More and more obviously, it seems to be located in that shady, little-known area where the human sense of norm is invaded by culture and shaped by its trends. Brenda has quickly learned that there are no more norms around, moral or rational. In a reality conceived by books, magazines and movies that command *not* to morally evaluate fornication, drug-induced bestiality, lack of any behavioral inhibition — killing becomes an antidote to boredom, a spectacle of figurines tipping over like on a TV screen.

Who, if anyone, can be blamed for that?

This is most likely the crucial question of our lifetime. Too many people, motivated by the best intentions, are doing away on a daily basis with Western fundamental values. They are busy creating the cultural climate according to certain gospels. With a closer look, we find out that they all fit into the general syndrome of the contemporary communication-entertainment complex. Which does not mean that the media and movie or publishing industries consist only of them.

What is cultural climate? And what are these gospels?

A cultural climate is an agglomeration of fashions, from philosophical to sartorial. Those from Schumpeter to Kristol who have written about the New Class, the intellectual and cultural establishments, the intelligentsia as social stratum, have paid too little attention to the fact that these power-hungry groups rule through fashion. As other establishments in history, they produce modes of behavior, attitudes and poses that determine their contemporaries, mold their existences and destinies. Present moods, trends and events together form a distinct cultural ambiance of our everydayness, and a more-or-less straight line could be traced from the Berkeley Free Speech Movement to Brenda Spencer. The sleazy subculture of the 60's has been made viable by the new concept of freedom stripped of any moral qualifications, which so easily transforms into crime, into lifestyles, and which, ultimately, ensconces cultural permissiveness as the reigning social and behavioral tenet. By now, we are in a trap: the natural balance between permission and prohibition has been demolished, prohibition has been declared evil per se, permission goodness per se. *That* kind of an idea, elevated to the status of a gospel by which people and society should live, is something that obviously invades mentalities and, finally, affects the very metabolism of a functioning society.

The American popular mind, so politically wayward and unpredictable, proves to be embarrassingly docile and timid versus cultural influences. A cultural climate is thus most effectively fabricated by the liberal culture's middle-echelon activists: editors, columnists, social commentators, feature writers, TV scriptwriters, critics (those same critics who care nothing about *Midnight Express'* sociocultural influence), reviewers, reporters, etc. It's thanks to them that someone like Mick Jagger is rewarded with $25 million for what they themselves call the message of "Excess, Threat and Androgyny." This gives a tremendous power to all those who manipulate culture on a mass scale. They display a fiery militant and investigative spirit wherever their preferences are at stake. They behave in an ominously ambiguous way when objectivity and good sense are badly needed. They declare what's good or bad by decree, unmotivated by any discernible moral or social criteria. Supported by them, any utterly mendacious movie, pernicious TV show, cynical novel, which has turned into a tremendous financial success, is bound to become a social factor, because the press and reviewers did nothing to thwart its cultural impact. Could a society survive holding up to its youth as exemplars "artistic" performers whose common denominator is an appalling amalgam of ruthlessness, meanness and mindlessness, blended together into a recipe for financial and social success? The answer to this question may be the key to our future, and as for now, the liberal culture is holding the key.

The most tragic and frightening aspect of the liberal culture's reign is that examples of complete decomposition of human instincts, as in Brenda's case, are almost instantly eradicated from the social awareness. It's an ominous portent for us all that all those exegetes, apologists and interpreters of everydayness in newspapers, magazines and TV newsrooms did not dwell on Brenda's exploits at all. Brenda's case seems to be forcibly and deliberately evicted from the pages of the press, eradicated from the public opinion's faculty to dwell on the horrors of life, and left only to the families of the victims to ponder over its moral and social meaning. Who could or should be held responsible for this?

CHAPTER 9

The Myth of the
Sexual Revolution*

Sexual Revolution is a pathetic misnomer. The most popular feature of revolutions is their reversal of roles: aristocrats go to the scaffold, judged by the wretched of the earth. The needy are told that all their needs will be fulfilled. The greedy have all their luxuries withdrawn—at least temporarily. In light of this simple recipe, nothing short of a mass impregnation of men by women would be enough of a sexual turnaround to justify the term revolution.

Revolutions are fomented by a mass dissatisfaction that engulfs a society and triggers violent outbreaks. If the sixties can be considered the beginning of the upheaval, history registers no previous tumult in the streets over the mass redistribution of sexual assets. What occurred was a change in attitudes—at first limited to a specific stratum of politically active intelligentsia, then transformed by the sensationalist-prone media into a cultural and behavioral trend. The media, as well as the entire opinion-making trade, were striving at exactly that time for a new role within the American civilization; they thus had a tremendous stake in the political proposition which was encapsulated in the slogan "make love not war." Boundless vistas suddenly opened before the new breed of American power-brokers—Manhattan's liberal press lords and publishers. Their hubris and hype in matters of sex, hitherto confined to abysmal trivialities, became—forthwith—endowed with ideology and dialectics. Within just a couple of years the subject had been appropriated not only from masters of Joycean caliber, Faulknerian gravity or even John O'Hara-like realistic bluntness, but also from the purveyors of sleazy Gothic prurience, à la Harold Robbins, and even from the peddlers of under-the-counter pornography. Ever since, sexualia has become a diversified industry in which pseudoscholarly littérateurs are rewarded not for insight but for fidelity to the line currently in vogue, and psychologists, sociologists and educators earn enormous sums for their endless proclamations of "findings" which are so trite and vulgar that even half a century ago they would have been laughed at in men's pubs by anyone over 18. The orgy of trampling the basic conventions and sensibilities of man-woman interrelationships has been going on now for almost two decades: it's not a revolution—it's a multibillion-dollar business.

But it also serves political purposes. Transvaluation of values, which often degenerates into nihilism, has always been a well-tested weapon of the political left: many times in history sexual customs have proved to be malleable by political subversion and manipulation. Eighteenth-century France and 19th-century Russia are excellent examples of how the dissolution of mores can serve political gains, how ideas of spurious egalitarianism and perverted freedom can benefit from being associated with the destruction of tenets that underlie sexual sensitivities—one of the most important human claims to betterness and civility. Yet, what is going on now in America somehow transcends political games: we are witnessing a different competition for power, one that goes beyond politics and aims at a more complete submission of man to doctrines. Therefore, putting worn-out labels—like secular humanism, liberal valuelessness or amoral radicalism—on the cynical promoters of sexual "liberation" won't do.

The phoniness of the term sexual "revolution" lies in the fact that it proposes nothing new—which is exactly what revolutions are supposed to do. The "prerevolutionary" American structure of sexual values was predicated on the chronic shortage of women on this continent; the residues of this long-forgotten sociodemographic condition were manifested, until recently, in what we still can see in old movies: men taking their hats off when a woman enters an elevator. The gist of the "revolution" can thus be grotesquely, but not unbelievably, summarized by what men now might take off when a woman enters a New York elevator, especially if some followers of punk lifestyles are already inside. (Some modish ads go even further and portray, perhaps not entirely unrealistically, what could happen to a young and handsome lift operator when an avowed feminist executive enters—and we are barely 20 years removed from *The Apartment,* a Billy Wilder movie, a touching love story on the theme of executives, elevators and their female operators.) Woman as a protected and respected combination of species *cum* symbol is out these days, extinguished by social theories, feminism and modish concepts of conduct; she's also out as an idiosyncratic component of a culture, a category for itself where conventional separateness determines customs and manners, but not the rudiments of existence. Thus, what happened to woman is not a revolution but the obliteration of a civilizational pattern. That does not change reality, merely impoverishes it.

The next casualty is sexuality's preciousness, uniqueness, its purely human quality, unknown in the animal world, which mates simply according to nature and season, without imbuing the procreative drive with any other sustaining contents.

There was always a good deal of robust lustiness in the fabric of American life and folklore, the natural vigor of men and women in a bountiful land of hard work, fearful dangers and cherished freedoms. Just like everywhere else, sexuality here was a source of passion, happiness, tragedy. The vitality and energy which became the national characteristics of Americans gave sexuality a sensationalist tinge which was particularly noticeable during the era of conquest, exploration and daring adventurousness of pioneer life. On the other hand, the excesses of individualism inherent in this social ambiance had to be regulated somehow by principles and precepts—the rigidity of which often resulted in conventions that were less normative than hypocritical.

Religion, which, in Europe, had tried for millennia to walk a tightrope between sexual morality and sexual mores, in America went head over heels into a direct confrontation—and the end result is our current chaos in which some American churches opt for modish permissive progressivism just to keep their flock in the pews, while others use obsolete dialectics to combat a permissiveness which they cannot comprehend. Actually, what Victorian arrangements in sexual manners did to America was to sublimate sexual satisfactions, which made their emotional texture different from, but probably more rewarding than, that of other cultures.

What the sixties did to American sexuality was to engender a sudden quantification, mass-popularization and trivialization of accepted practices. Revolution means qualitative change, the introduction of *something*—the birth of an idea, a technological breakthrough, a new concept of interrelationships between people—but nothing of this sort occurred. No new reality was invented. What happened was a recrafting of sexual postures which were well known from other junctures of history. Human sexual conduct (so it was said) needed no norms of any kind; an increased volume of sexual activity is an indication of personal freedom which reforms the social order; men and women should reject criteria of sexual etiquette in order to become better, more human; a life improved is a life in which sexual casualness mercilessly evicts reverence for and exceptionality of the sexual experience; mass-produced values for sexual acts advance social progress; perfunctory sexual engagements determine a higher consciousness; scientists, writers and social pundits (the consciences of our time) have full license to inject normlessness into society at their convenience.

There was nothing new in this concept of sexuality—what *Playboy* announced as novel had been practiced by Eve in the first version of the Club Mediterrannée, a much more lush rendition than any subsequent one. What the puny commercial hustlers pushed in America as a sexual revolution was old hat in Sodom. However, there was one new factor—the mass media and the entertainment industry, which thrived on presenting these worn-out notions as dizzying revelations. The news that "everything goes," for adults and juveniles alike, was, for the peddlers of pop culture and "lifestyles," similar to the California gold rush. The way they plugged into that boom turned the quantity coefficient into a herd instinct. Universal permission for the young to plunge into sexual activity, sanctioned by the media's quotidian omnipresence in all channels of the cultural spectrum, brought about a monstrous increase in the overall volume of fornication. Unprejudiced students were always aware of the fact that the volume was a varying matter: people always did *it* rather profusely; what was changing was the attitude toward information about those practices—the intensity and frequency of their widespread visibility. Periods of hecticality, passivity and constraint have alternated throughout history, modified by religions, moral climates, socioeconomic preoccupations, mythologies. One thing is observable: although those who argued for the relaxation of sexual mores and for blunt openness about them *claimed* to foster society's health and happy stability, mankind always seemed to flourish most—socially and culturally—during eras of prudery, hypocrisy and regimentation. Empires and wealth were built on sexual conventions, and their demise was always signaled by the "wholesome" abolition of those conventions and the accepted dissolution of sexual comportment.

The journalists' ignorant hype—the scourge of our epoch and the yeast of the liberal press's omnipotence—proclaimed a revolution that never took place. The daily-communication racket has structured a reality in which new taboos, idols, mental constructs and habits are fabricated. The tone of journalistic enunciations on things sexual in the *New York Times, Time* magazine and on CBS is, in essence, the same coinage of clichés as the medieval obscurantist preacheries about the interaction between the devil and carnality—in a diametrically opposite sense, of course. When a silver-haired obstetrician who represents Planned Parenthood argues on television for juvenile access to contraceptives and abortion *without* parental consent and who predicts that to refuse these adolescent "civil rights" will result in an America engulfed by a cataclysm of teen-age pregnancies, we have a surrealistic inversion of the free-will principle—namely that human sexual destiny does not belong to a person (his or her individual qualities, existential priorities, emotions, ties, bonds, etc.) but to a bureaucratized, allegedly scientific "Providence" whose supreme ontological force—called "research"—holds ultimate sway over human fate.

What has the introduction of the term "sexual revolution," and all the social symptoms connected to it, done to everyday life?

Those segments of society which accepted that philosophy—predominantly the mobile urban liberal intelligentsia of the last generation—are very likely to have sustained psychological and biological damages whose dimensions are still unmeasurable. We are looking at the slogan "buy now, pay later" transplanted into the realm of delicate moral and emotional membranes. We've all heard about hippie communes which reactivated venereal diseases believed to have been extinct for centuries. A woman, contrary to feminist allegations, is more vulnerable to license institutionalized by fashion than a man is, both physiologically and mentally, and she more easily falls prey to situational ethics and the void of criteria. The nineteen eighties will bring an incipient awareness of the later payments which will be due from the women who bought the stereotypes of the "revolution" in the seventies—the facts of life and their renditions in literature will tell us what happened to the women who purchased the pristine shamelessness and the "wholesome" atrophy of standards. We are already beginning to hear about the gnawing feelings of emptiness that are inherent in any existence divorced from life's basic and inescapable truths. The main culprit, of course, is the liberal communication complex which, over two decades, merely "reported what was taking place" and "what people wanted"—according to the words of a *New York Times* editor. The testimony of the press's grim role probably will never sink into the American public's consciousness, and the media's mendacity will triumph once again with the homily, "we do not create social climates or cultural moods—we reflect them," which, of course, is the century's most ghastly lie. Beginning with the *Times,* this benign promotion of sexual nihilism trickles down to every local paper in the country, democratizing the ancient rot of moneyed classes into the shabby, cheap licentiousness of the provincia.

Thus, the "revolution" has proved to be little more than soiling the nation's cultural fabric. Since the commercial exploitation of sex and the political rip-off syndrome are inseparable, the brutalization of sexual sentiments will ultimately produce inferior and shoddier Americans of both genders—and there are sinister forces both within our society and abroad which are profoundly interested in exactly that consequence. The perverted First Amendment is perhaps the most painful casualty in this development: it's doubtful that Jefferson intended it to protect *Hustler* magazine. And who knows how many of us will pay dearly for the collusion of corrupted "sexologists" with ruthless media entrepreneurs who, in the name of liberal progress, have dismantled some of man's and woman's most reliable supports for their forming of mankind together?

CHAPTER 10

Sexometrics*

The concerted effort to "solve" sexual problems with the help of statistics and scientific research, has a practical value of seeking to provide an automatic dispenser for human destinies. Such efforts have multiplied from Freud and Havelock Ellis on through Kinsey, Van der Velde and Masters and Johnson, down to the numerous cohort of feminists and quacks. I believe that both science and pseudoscience have improved nothing in this sphere and that the human sexual universe is as enigmatic and vulnerable today as ever. However, the labors of honest scientists and charlatans alike have indeed had a result: human sexuality has been submerged in triteness, paltriness, vagueness and vulgarity to an extent unknown before. The most ruthless hawkers of the sexual rubbish in mankind's history have been legitimized by a bizarre cooperation between science and "science" in the pages of popular magazines. In the absence of an effective defense weapon, a limitless escalation of abomination and degeneracy in the pursuit of ever new thrills has come gradually to determine our culture.

Not long ago, the Illinois newspapers began to carry headlines: "The Sexual Abuse of Children!" or "Child Porn Rampant in America!" One might suppose this to be a phenomenon of street-level depravity, or the jaded rich. But in 1975, the Saint Martin Press, a respectable Manhattan firm, published an album entitled *Show Me*, which has been prominently displayed on the New York elite's coffee tables ever since. In it, a psychiatrist and teacher, together with an acclaimed photographer, undertook a thoughtless and repulsive incursion into the world of juvenile sensibilities. In glossy, suggestive photographs, 10 to 14 year olds of both genders adopt lascivious poses, mutually examine genitals, try desperately to imitate the adult world in its normal endeavors and sensations, which at their age is blatantly abnormal, faked, full of sham. The book ". . . is an explicit, thoughtful and affectionate picture book designed to satisfy children's curiosity about sex and sexuality — their own as well as that of their elders . . ." — says the blurb, which also provides the endorsements of a director of the New York Medical College, the Unitarian/Universalist Association of Churches, the *San Francisco Chronicle* and *Examiner*, and Wilson Library Bulletin. In the text, Western society is repeatedly denounced as still "repressive," even though a short stroll through some New York City streets would make a tourist from Gommorah blush. We read there too: ". . . Embraces and caresses (of the genitals) are fun and pleasurable for both children and adults . . . ," and I can't help asking: What is the difference between a scientist who condones the sexual arousal of adults

*Taken from the article "The Glandular Stench in America" which appeared in *The Rockford Papers*, April, 1977 (Vol. 2, No. 3) issue.

by children and vice versa, and the knave who psychically and physically abuses children when filming *Lollytots*? However, scientists whose sense of responsibility is difficult to recognize keep advising America on TV talk shows, lionized there by demi-intelligent hosts who seem to fear that common sense will result in a decline in Nielsen ratings. A strange alliance between scholars and garbage mongers is producing a breeding ground for vice, inconceivable in former ages.

However, the worst that is wrought upon youth by *Show Me* is its truculent destruction of children's unique quest for hidden meanings of sexuality which they do not want to have programmed by adults like a school curriculum. Adults may know more about arithmetic and social obligations, but they have forgotten rewards that come from one's solitary groping for explanations, from one's own handling of the pre-puberty anxieties. What both sexual scientists and sexual witch doctors pursue is their collectivist censorship of the individual and imaginative exploration of mysteries; even if this search is so painfully short-lived, the sexologists hate every bit of its sanctity and secretiveness. Countless polls reveal, actually, the youth's longing for a firm code of behavior. The adults, obsessed with "reform," do not want to acknowledge the polls. The authors of *Show Me* enforce on children their preconceived, theoretical regulations which are meant to sanction their fictitious sexual "revolution."

*   *   *

Many say: "Another Rome, decline, decadence, collapse—" The similarity is striking, but between Rome and now there have been Christianity, gothic cathedrals, Dante, humanism, Shakespeare, Rembrandt, the American Constitution, Beethoven and Einstein. A pornographic heat wave is no match for such an accumulation of values, but it appears that the civilized forms of existence retreat before massage parlors, the mindless radical chic of *Harper's Bazaar*, the robber barons who enrich themselves selling pictures of orifices, the female novelists who trumpet their demands to be both unwashed and desired. The vitiated tradition of liberty says: "Let's ignore it! It will bottom out, abate by itself, peter out, ebb out . . ." That's an illusion. Untreated funguses, discharges and sores do not disappear by themselves. They grow and contaminate the organism, weaken it so that it succumbs to disease. What has already been irretrievably lost, at least for one generation, is the sense of sexual diginity based on reticence and restraint which provides more than one dimension for a meaningful life. Sexual taste, seemliness, self-respect, even at a price of deprivation, are components of sexual elation, happiness, pride — words that soon may be eradicated from the vocabulary of sexual emotions, concepts that soon may vanish from our understanding. The mass parade of sexual paraphernalia will erode the sense of exceptionality — and it's hard to imagine how a society can survive without this scope of our minds. An entire generation, afflicted by the bombardment of sexologists and smut peddlers, has been sentenced to torporific and uglier life, although it does not know it yet. It will discover it later, with an all-pervading feeling of emptiness in their hearts.

There seems to be little choice for those who care about human imaginative sanctuaries other than to resort to law. A lawful distinction has to be made between the power of a picture and the power of a word, so that the ardors and torments that shaped the abundance of the human experience over millennia are not killed by anyone who owns a printing press and a camera and has enough money to abuse the First Amendment with the help of lawyers and casuistry.

Every state and every community in America should have the right to impose censorship of the pictorial presentations of sexuality. The claim that it would endanger culture is preposterous. Gambling is prohibited in many places but permitted in Nevada: whoever lusts for gambling may go to Las Vegas. Pornography may be permanently ensconced on 42nd Street and Sunset Strip — whoever finds it necessary may pilgrim to those Meccas. The argument that if prohibited, pornography will sell under the counter is self-defeating: it is exactly where pornography belongs, where it fits into social reality. It is its legality that makes it devastating, not its illegality.

We seem to sit in a beautiful living room comforted by sophisticated technology and admirable works of art, while in the very middle of the imposing interior an enormous heap of excrement befouls the air we breathe. Some pretend to ignore it and fan themselves with lofty and learned treatises on civil rights, the First Amendment, the ambivalences of liberty. Others claim that such an atmosphere is salubrious. Still others believe that words like "Tolerance" or "Progress" will do away with stench if incessantly repeated. No one dares to reach for a shovel because the liberal culture has declared it filthier than the grounds of fetidness, and—at the same time—a taboo. But the putridness will not be removed without a tool. So the choice is between an unprepossessing action and choking to death.

In an age when Harvard University students have access to *A Student Guide to Sex on Campus* as well as a course catalog, people's right to decency must ask law and law enforcement for support. Some think it impossible to preserve democracy and eradicate rot, but de Tocqueville wrote: "Impossibility is considered a challenge in America . . ."

CHAPTER 11

Normalcy — Our Sixth Sense*

What's normalcy?

No one knows exactly. People with an innate propensity for moody incertitude would argue that, to begin with, it does not exist. Both scientists and sophist philosophers are uneasy with it: it is somehow counter to the on-the-other-hand recipe for knowledge. On the other hand, however, without the notion of normalcy, both science and casuistry would turn into sports of irrationality turned loose, which they can hardly afford. Thus, a biologist might argue that normalcy is 68° Fahrenheit, that is a temperature in which many organisms best grow and prosper. It's a cogent definition, though useless outside of a laboratory. Nature is known for never having produced two identical limbs, minds or rocks. So how can we speak of one standard applicable to love, democracy, sophistication, compassion or sense of humor?

As normalcy was not provided by nature, we had to do something about it. We discovered early that the lack of normality in the universal scheme was a defect, and we had to correct it. We felt its need. So, we invented it. We thought it up; it was necessary for us to have a measure of viable order, indispensable for living in a community, in a society, or just peaceably one next to another. Thus, its possible absence at the moment of creation is not proof of its nonexistence. It exists now just as the internal combustion engine, aspirin, differential calculus and the State Department.

So — what's normalcy?

It is a standard, or a set of standards, applicable and acceptable to most, to the largest amount of people. A rather primitive exemplification: most people react adversely to noxious smells. But both medicine and literature teach us that there are some people who cull an unexpected bliss from sniffing odors the majority of mankind abhors. We call the first response normal and the second unusual, extraordinary, or interesting, if we are either very hip or very polite. We may call it abnormal.

For centuries, normalcy — as a notion, a word and a practical frame of reference for arts and sciences — generated little excitement, or even interest. It was a concept which we could deduct from data offered to us by reasoning, empiricism, observation. Sages might have nursed some suspicions about its precise meaning, but they did not consider it urgent to probe and dissect it. Not long ago, however, the post-Einsteinian natural sciences fractured the very notion of normalcy without abrogating its necessity. With the arrival of

*Editorial in *Chronicles of Culture*, September/October 1979. (Vol. 3, No. 5)

institutionalized psychology and psychoanalysis, normalcy fell into disgrace.

For a hundred-odd years, the doctors of psyche have been waging a merciless and murderous war of extinction against normalcy. They call it the worst names and swear not to rest until it is totally eradicated from our minds, feelings and bodies; our primary need to relate to something more stable and solid than dreams, drives and dreads seems to the psychoanalysts unwholesome. The animus against normalcy on the part of those learned in dealing with murky impulses may be grounded in their faithfulness to science's honor, to the results of their research, and in speculations which make them conclude that normalcy is a false, or at least spurious, presumption. But many wonder whether it is the purity of scientific freedom that is at stake. Many of us see normalcy not only as something complex and enigmatic, but also as something both utilitarian and idealistic, pragmatic and visionary in the same breath — in a word: something much too weighty to be left to psychologists to decide. "I am positive I have a soul; nor can all the books with which materialists have pestered the world ever convince me to the contrary—" Laurence Sterne wrote when the spiritual equipment had been rabidly denied to humans by the militants of the 18th-century antisoul movement. Billions of people on this planet are equally positive that normalcy exists — and, moreover, that it is indispensable for a sense of eventual survival in the world of today, where the norms of human values and cogent human endeavors are gleefully shattered by the social elites gone nihilist and by the liberal media which support them. People have a burning desire to preserve the virtue of blushing when obscenities are spread around, and to expect an "Excuse me—" when bumping into each other. They yearn to call this state of things normalcy, while calling the disposition or conduct of those who tend to do away with blushing and civility abnormal.

Thus, during all those millennia when we lived with normalcy as a welcome and admired partner, it became more than a word, a notion, a point of reference. It has now become our sixth sense. As we know them, human senses are distinguished by the circumstance that most people have them in common —though not all of the people; much as we wish that everybody could see, there are the sightless among us. We may be aware that it's immensely hard to define the sense of normalcy, but it is possible. It is a sense which is close to taste and touch, with a wide range of differentiated preferences. We all know that at a certain point, the amount of hotness in a dish can reach a degree at which even the most enthusiastic afficionado of spiced food will find personal offense. Not long ago, America's newspapers obtrusively peddled the story of a youthful homosexual who decided to take a homosexual date to his high school prom. The adolescent deviate was not off the mark as far as his correct gauging of the sociocultural climate of his age is concerned: we live in times of the hypertrophy of a peculiar mood of tolerance, when every excess or abuse of the sense of normalcy is tolerated, while a free opinion about those abuses is not. He can hardly be called a nonconformist, as his was an act of compliance with the reigning behavioral dogma, a collaboration with power, not a challenge of power, as the homosexuals are simply an officially sanctioned social minority these days, thanks to the decree of liberal culture and fashion. Thus, the young inverts gained entrance to festivities in keeping with the new social mood, but, according to press reports, people started to leave when they appeared. No one was hostile or repressive, but their manifested union offended something in everybody. Everybody's sense of normalcy was hurt.

That's obvious to anyone with unatrophied common sense. It is far from obvious to homosexuals and all those who see a civil rights cause in sexual deviation. At the very core of the contemporary homosexual crusade is a claim to normalcy. The rest of mankind, or one should say the overwhelming majority of mankind, cannot and will never accept this as either justified or true. Normalcy in the realm of sexuality is the duality of genders, which conditions procreation, which guarantees the continuity of life. Anything that contradicts this fundamental scheme cannot *also* be normal, lest words lose their meaning and interhuman communication cease. A physical digression from the standard is ailment or sickness, which we regard as a temporary absence of the normal functions of the body. However, nothing seems more unacceptable to a homosexual than calling his disposition a sickness: he does not consider himself infirm in any way, and perhaps with good reason. Thus, we have a lingering conflict, whose essence is the sense of normalcy and its vicissitudes, in an era when understanding, compassion and even indulgence no longer assuage human grievances; normalcy must be abused and trampled in order to redress injustices or errors of the past. And this abuse gravely distorts our ability to build a society and create social moods where comity, humanness and genuine tolerance can flourish and benefit us all.

Whatever the bickering of modern psychoshamans who never will acquiesce to normality as a verifiable phenomenon, most people would repeat Laurence Sterne's words deep down in the soul, chiefly because normalcy is no longer a notion from the realm of psychology, anthropology, physics or medicine. In our time, it has become a moral concept — today it determines both our distinction between right and wrong, and our ethical choices. Only in such a perspective can we correctly perceive feminism not as an idea, but as an affirmative action on behalf of those who are wronged either by nature or society; as such it has all the irrational features of affirmative actions that are movements of the heart rather than the mind, whatever their source of destination. When Freud first suggested that normalcy and sanity were relative impressions of the human mind, many were apprehensive whether — even assuming that his findings were true — a society, let alone a civilization, could be structured on such a discovery. But Freud was still a man of intellectual tact: those who read him properly soon conclude that authentic Freudism is only a system of suspicions. His epigones began to relentlessly press down the pedal, and now, thanks to the social results of their efforts, many see clearly that normalcy and sanity are moral preconditions for our very survival. Deviations and aberrations can be commiserated and alleviated, but accepting them as a coeval principle of a social order spells suicide. However, our premonitions and our will to cope with the misguided legacy of Freud have been rendered moot by the unexpected twist of cultural moods. Hysterics and neuroses have fled the boundaries of scientific studies and have invaded the rolling landscapes of literature and literary fads; they have quickly turned into shallow poses and fashions among the elites and, smoothly blended with phony egalitarianism, have begun to infect the masses. By the second part of the century, the reigning cultural modes had alacritously agreed to draw an equal sign between normalcy and abnormalcy: whoever simply declared himself and his proposals normal and sane easily acquired the stamp of normalcy and sanity from the liberal culture, regardless of any criteria of reason, objectivity, logic or experience. Acts and events followed profusely, and suddenly we found ourselves in a reality whose spokespersons held it utterly unbecoming to maintain that both Charles Manson and Gore Vidal thrive on insanity. To express a view that the Woodstock subculture bred abnormalcy was the ultimate in bad manners, let alone taste. Any demand that a commonly obligatory principle of human existence be upheld was called repression in psychology and oppression in national affairs. Sexual chaos, erratic bestiality of man toward man, the dissipation of the social fabric and a dismal cheapening of the quality of life duly ensued.

One of the major wishes of human mind and heart is for a coherence of wishes and attainments. As every ideal, this coherence is hard to reach: we are by nature neither white nor black but a sort of composite greyish. However, an overtly proclaimed renunciation of striving toward coherence, and replacing it with the disjointment of personal exertions and endeavors, is an invitation to abnormality, and gives it special powers to regulate existence. It is soon transformed into a lethal threat to the assorted stabilities and securities that form the basis for an organized society. Certainly, some would say: "So what?" but most will respond: "Wait and see..." The subculture of the mid-'60s injected huge masses with an aberrant conviction that youth was the center of one's life span and no one should bother about what might happen later. It resulted in a generation unable to project itself as becoming older in its preferences and propensities. Just one adolescent who was so limited could easily be disregarded as a juvenile idiot, but a mass of people imbued with this same persuasion produced what was perhaps the largest abuse of peacetime normalcy in history.

It may be difficult to understand, much less to accept, but our strength and weekness, our vitality and our debilitation are geared to the proper functioning of our sense of normalcy. The vigorousness of our belief in the normative categories of our feelings and our conduct precede any consideration of whether or not our institutions and our social organism are still viable. We must feel bound by those normative forces accumulated in ourselves, in our traditions and customs. The New American Person created by the liberal culture does not feel obligated by such forces: he/she may still believe that law and morality play some little-specified role in a society, but they accept normlessness and abnormalcy in the name of "higher" necessities or moralities. We who think of oursleves as nonliberals do not.

Normalcy is a cornerstone of our worldview. On occasion, our faith in normalcy makes us underdogs. More often it constitutes our bridge to people who do not comprehend too well our nomenclatures and harangues about philosophy, morality and their relation to social health, which is so much better exemplified by remedies for inflation and the energy crisis. But when we read some polls, we know how close we are to the mainstream of the American mass thinking that articulates itself by rejecting abnormalcy. *Playboy* magazine, which fancies itself as having created a new subculture of fast food hedonism designed to anesthetize the midlife blues, polled its readers not long ago, with the Harris Company's help, and found that notions like noncarnal love, fidelity and marriage still hold an inexplicable spell over the great majority of them. To the smart intellectualoids in *Playboy's* headquarters those findings were both enigmatic and loathesome: their cultural limitations bar them from knowing that their "philosophy" has been privy to mankind since the first realization that humans mate regardless of seasons, that the consequence of coupling is not always procreation, and the random sex reduces the worth of life so much that it makes it vegetatively meaningless and boring. We thus invented the sexual principles of love, custom, convention, chastity, modesty, normalcy.

Superb civilizations and cultures were structured on these exclusively human devices; life became meaningful, rich, full of purely human happiness and sadness, without whose interplay we would be little different from gnats. Now, *Playboy* ideologists have come up with a proposition of the one-night-stand sexual ethos, once quite popular with cavemen and practiced by drifting misfits throughout the history of mores and marvel that their customers may pay for gawking but are reluctant to make such supermarket wisdom a guiding theory of life.

So, while we are noting public opinion surveys, it would make sense to report that one, recently undertaken on behalf of the Illinois General Assembly, found that 71% of the people interviewed were in favor of dropping insanity as a legal defense for a crime. If this is not a dramatic, poignant outcry for restoration of the notion of normalcy as an obligatory coefficient of social reality — then I don't know what is. I only hope that more and more people will start thinking how to wisely institutionalize these overbearing sentiments of so many of us.

CHAPTER 12

Our Civilization*

*". . . And above all it is **your** civilization, it is **you**. However much
you hate it or laugh at it, you will never be happy away from it for
any length of time . . . Good or evil, it is yours, you belong to it,
and this side of the grave you will never get away from the marks it
has given you —"* George Orwell

Hating and laughing at a civilization is as old as civilization itself. Most who
hate and laugh wind up, later on in life, with a feeling of having been
hoodwinked, or stupid—an unpleasant sensation. To warn them that their
youthful hatred and rebellious jeers are traps is, however, all but impossible
because they're impenetrable to rational argumentation.

Our epoch had, and still has, its share of hating and jeering. To anyone of
sensible disposition, Orwell's words would indicate that civilization is a gratifying gift, yet many are scarcely aware of its existence in and around themselves. We Americans are particularly fortunate as participants in something
of rare worth—the American civilization. Because it is conferred upon him as
a natural condition, the average American is not conscious of what it means to
be born into it; many of us, confused by the existential din so benumbing in
America, are routinely induced to view our civilization as an undeserved
calamity.

In fact, the American civilization is a value, both human and humane to an
extent unknown to other civilizations. It is a source of our strength and
weaknesses, virtues and sins, achievements and failures. But above all, it is
ours and it shapes us every hour of life. We often fail to recognize how much
the rest of the world envies us our civilization, tries jealously to imitate us at
each step. Even those of other nations who claim that they don't want our
civilization, pursue a path of eager emulation, whereas those who openly hate
us burn American flags and libraries while donning American blue jeans,
refreshing themselves with Coca Cola, and singing songs of revolt which come
to them directly from American folk music. And this is an American triumph
so momentous and unique that its impact is still difficult to assess.

For a long time it has been known that a civilization can be an originator of
patriotism, but nowhere before so pointedly clear as it is in America. Some
believe the correlation between patriotism and civilization is a mark of materialism, close to corruption, but the opposite is true. Patriotism grounded in
haughtiness and an impulse to conquer is of dubious quality; patriotism
derived from lofty sentiments may ennoble the soul and help literature; but
love of country stemming from a pragmatic, though instinctual, recognition
that one's country is a cradle of a rewarding civilization is a source of

voluntary, thus precious, social cohesion. An exiled poet, bitterly disappointed in America after President Roosevelt had delivered Eastern Europe to the Stalinist thralldom, described the following scene from the postwar forties: In the scorching New York heat, a man in rags is digging into the Manhattan rock with a pick; it is a killing labor but the man ebulliently sings in some Slavic language; approached by the poet, he informs him that he is a Ukrainian, just arrived on these shores, speaks no English, works fourteen hours a day to earn enough to bring his family over from Europe; asked why, in such dire condition, he feels like singing, he makes a broad gesture which includes the famous New York skyline and says. "I'm in America! It's all mine!" The poet, taking leave, is under the impression of having met a primitive mind which still naively believes in the old American clichés; then it dawns on him what an intuitive depth was in the Ukrainian's exclamation: the man sensed, rather than understood the gist of the American civilization — namely that it is the property of anyone who embraces it. A man such as he may be destitute, but nobody makes him a lesser man because he doesn't know the native tongue as would occur everywhere else, and he gets such good pay for his heavy toil as would occur nowhere else. By stepping into America, he has acquired freedom from tyranny and a personal economic value — both prime elements of a successful civilization. He becomes an instant patriot, an American specialty which easily becomes devotion to and fierce faith in American principles.

To many aficionados of fashionable persuasions, the words of a black American behavioral scientist, published some time ago in *The New York Times*, certainly sound like blasphemy. He wrote that according to an *Ebony* magazine poll ". . . the great majority of blacks considered this country worth defending against foreign enemies," and that ". . . still another survey found that more than three-quarters of the blacks describe themselves as 'sick and tired' of hearing attacks on 'traditional American values'." The upsurge of black American patriotism directly after the violent sixties, during which the ultimate and inevitable tearing apart of the nation into two implacably hostile racial groups seemed a foregone conclusion, is a far-reaching evolution. According to the blatant and powerful stereotype — the modish gospel of the last decade — the young black American could only hate American civilization, the alleged source of all his miseries. But then we see him on millions of TV screens, as we did recently after he won an Olympic medal in boxing, putting his hand to his heart during the national anthem, and we hear him saying that, oblivious of his paralyzing injuries, he had fought for "Davey, my parents, my girl friend, and all the people of the United States . . ." We can thus safely maintain that in spite of our inadequacies, in no society on this planet is the love of the country so intricately interwoven with both the civilizational heritage and promise as it is in America. Black American patriotism is a magnificent point scored, but in fact, nothing new in this land. Those who for centuries have watched America from afar were always fascinated by a peculiar American phenomenon — the intense and heartfelt flourishing of American patriotism among simple, impecunious, often downtrodden people who always know better how to love, respect and appreciate America than most of those who have derived wealth from her, and perhaps therefore hold her in low esteem — their own vile, self-devouring notion of spiritual luxury.

* * *

I believe that two basic ingredients account for our civilization's glory: the power of reason, which warrants our freedoms, and the sense of responsibility, which justifies their social and individual use. We inherited these concepts in a larger package, commonly called Western civilization. In it, the Hebrews saw a regulatory might in reason, and the supreme moral norm in man's responsibility to God; the Hellenes explored reason and responsibility as cast against the riddles of fate; Christianity fused them with love and metaphysics into an overpowering needs of the human soul. Then we Americans endowed them with an irresistibility that inculcated our civilization into the universal awareness.

For centuries, mankind has been spellbound by America: in the beginning, there was the magnitude of landscape and the romanticism of pioneering, then the exuberance of human and social possibilities, never known to the rest of the world on such scale. Later, the world fixed its gaze on Gary Cooper's gait and listened with rapt attention to Louis Armstrong's trumpet. America's fairy tales and mystifications became global cultural fare, its folklore global elegance, its sufferings and grievances, transmitted through art and literature, a global concern. As of now, mankind knows more about American myths and presidents than about anything else of historical and public significance.

With reason and responsibility as fundamental values, the American civilization achieved a wealth of thought patterns and forms of life unknown to other civilizations. A reality of galactic complexity and matching openness has been created. It evolved social textures and concepts of civic liberty, dignity and duty which have made man proud of himself. History proves that where reason and responsibility prevail, a great civilization, in spite of all adversities, corrosions and long duration of due changes, will prosper and implement justice. Once reason and responsibility cease to prevail, the greatness of the civilization fades away.

* * *

Contrary to nineteenth-century materialist, positivist and marxist preachings, our century has already proven that a civilization is determined by its culture more than by its economy and its politics. If knife, fork and spoon are civilization, someone wrote, the way of using them is culture. In our age of Telstar satellites, this instrumental *how* becomes omnipotent and indicates that if civilization is a source of power, culture is a source of power within a civilization. No one seems to know more about this force nowadays than Americans.

Unfortunately, culture has often tended to be scornful of civilization. Beginning with Rousseau, a sequence of cautious thinkers including Mark Twain, Anatole France and Bernard Shaw has indulged in speculating on the borderline situations that demonstrate how easily the veneer of civilization can be shed off by civilized man. In our lifetime, the Nazis and the communists have actually shown how easy it is to abandon even the elemental vestiges of civilizational heritage. However, in democratic societies, culture has tended to cooperate with civilization. Why the two are now in sharp conflict in America is difficult to ascertain. It is an enigma why children of a generation that won for America a selfless and righteous war, and then performed deeds of singular generosity toward the rest of the world, should be filled with anti-American passions, presumably directed against American greed and exploitation of other peoples. The fact is that by the end of the sixties, we found ourselves involved in a civil war of principles and values, infinitely more crucial than any struggle with outside nations. Any external assault seems anemic when compared with the disintegration or moral and social bonds which is now taking place.

What are the origins of this contest? Historically, it starts with culture's attack on reason and responsibility, which can be traced to the beginnings of the nineteenth century. Powerful movements of ideas began to erode Western values, charging them with barrenness and inhuman rigidity. In recent times, those who prefer to discard them accuse our civilization of a sinful lack of compassion and assert a new definition of freedom which will eliminate the traditional restraints of reason and responsibility as detrimental to human progress. The very core of their postulates is to do away with limitation as a positive and useful notion, both in civilization and culture. Thus, the front lines emerge, positions are drawn. The contemporary contention seems to be:
—between what today is called id, ego, or the subconscious, as opposed to reason;
—between conscience as opposed to responsibility;
—between the common sense of social instincts as opposed to culture (as culture is conceived by the intellectual elites that rule it nowadays).
But is culture a homogeneous entity, a unified camp in open warfare with other forms of human activities? Certainly not. Culture is too great a notion, and it encompasses too many factors and values to be ceded without struggle to a single directive.

*   *   *

In order to save culture, we must be aware of what endangers it. These are the threats:

—The unilateral equating of limitation with evil is a false truth, both philosophically and logically. It leads to dissolution of the social and individual sense of law, responsibility, duty and justice — all essential pillars of our civilization. We see around us license presented as virtue, condoning irrational permissiveness in ethics and civic affairs, and destroying the relationship between the sexes and generations. This social mood subverts all forms of organized life.

—The facile pseudohumanism, which recommends unqualified and disjointed pseudofreedoms, degrades the human person from the central site of human dignity down to the hodge-podge of the pocketbook psychology, fraudulently adulated as today's moral salvation.

—The efforts to reduce the broad range of norms, evolved by the Judeo-Christian ethos, to the single concept of individual conscience — a noble but slippery category of thinking and feeling — are not improving but banefully impoverishing our civilization and ourselves.

—The deliberate subordination of man's accumulated wisdom and knowledge to a mechanically administered scientism, and the tendency to present the discipline of mind and heart, the cornerstone of human integrity, as inferior to attitudes and behavior responding to amorphous impulses, are ominous steps toward decline.

—The conviction, now dominant in the communication media, that the presentation of information about evil will diminish evil — assuming, for instance, that if Charles Manson were to write a best-seller, give interviews, and lecture about his crimes, he would thus prove himself a benefit for mankind and not a bestial scourge — is one of the most foreboding fallacies of our time.

—The assertion that the terror of radical ideas and of wanton political violence is less immoral and inflicts less wrong on freedom, democracy and civilization than the lawful attempt to prevent and combat such activities, may spell our own demise.

—The inane tyranny of faddishness that looks up to exotic faiths and philosophies, which dolefully failed to provide their own civilizations and peoples with liberty, dignity and justice, as answers to our civilization's deficiencies, is one of our civilization's portentous follies.

* * *

The fact that the body of ideas cited above is being promoted, and its impact is noticeable in America, is beyond question. However, to establish a link between ideas and people and their influences is a delicate matter. In current nomenclatures, what generates the ideas we oppose is sometimes called the liberal culture, or the permissive culture, or the fasionable orthodoxy. Those terms, of course, lack precision but they are not removed from actuality. The people who stand behind them tend to call themselves liberals. They adopt the superiority of permissiveness over restraint as an article of faith. Their proc-lamations are instantly turned by the mass media into a cultural fashion zealously imposed upon society by dint of repetition. If we only realize that during the last ten years, no one who has tried to advance ideas contrary to their philosophy has received the Pulitzer Prize or the National Book Award — the two most widely publicized honors of the American culture —the need for an intellectual counter-force becomes obvious. The reigning cultural establishment which must be challenged consists of compatriots who think differently than nonliberals do. Thus, the other voice which should be offered in accordance with the tenets of a pluralistic society will, I hope, be welcomed in the everlasting dialogue which seems indispensable for the future of the American civilization. I assume that the liberals want to make America better, just as I do. What I expect is that nonliberal ideas and endeavors be met with the same good will as I'm prepared to meet the beliefs of others.

*   *   *

The postulate that reason, responsibility and social necessity for limitations on individual conduct are, in a free country, morally and socially superior to unbridled permissiveness is often labeled a superstition. I happen to think these concepts to be more progressive, audacious and sophisticated than the current prejudice against them. For many centuries, various cultures have been fascinated by the human being's private hell, but until now, no culture has considered the nonstop display of private hells as socially beneficial. On the contrary, an awareness of their complexity, and an effort to keep such matters private in order not to impose one's burden upon others, was consi-dered a basic virtue. Today, as its proudest banner, the permissive culture promulgates "Hanging it out!"—that is, an endless parade of private hells in literature, arts, behavioral sciences, mass media and entertainment. Moreover, private hells gone public, in spite of the obvious commercial spuriousness of most of them, have been declared a mark of individual value as well as social boon, salutary for the common good. Any suggestion to limit this gush of psychic secretions and deformations which, in my view, has a socially pollut-ing effect, is currently decried as an assault on constitutional freedoms.

Nothing dramatizes better this situation than the following note in *Time* magazine, itself a factory of mass-produced permissive thinking:

"Milestones

Died: Morris L. Ernst, 87, civil liberties and labor lawyer who served as an advisor to U.S. Presidents, in New York City. Ernst had a passion for causes, and very few were lost. An ebullient foe of censorship, he broke down the ban on James Joyce's *Ulysses*. He served as counsel to the American Civil Liberties Union; he defended Communists and Frank Costello, while deploring both. Concerned in later life that too many restraints had been removed, he declared that he would not want "to live in a society without limits to freedom."

Time didn't specify where Mr. Ernst had made his statement, nor what the trajectory of thinking that had brought a model American liberal to such a fateful inference. This short epitaph is a shattering argument. If someone who successfully devoted his life to the defense of the liberal concept of freedom bitterly confesses, in his twilight years, that the fruit of his work is sour, something must be wrong with that which he had worked for.

I understand and respect the poignancy of Morris Ernst's admission. I firmly believe that freedom divorced from reason and responsibility is no longer freedom but freedom's reverse, which ultimately must turn against the American civilization and consequently, against man and mankind. But the American civilization is in for still more trouble unless a New Reformation, rooted in reason and responsibility, becomes the chief agent of its culture. A crucial battle between two concepts of American democracy is ravaging the country and our lives. It is a struggle between America-as-civilization and America-as-society. A democratic civilization abides by commandments and principles; its freedoms, privileges and benefits are conditioned by a sustained and obliging sense of duties, ethics and rules of conduct. A democratic society asks primarily for the right to be fragmented according to disparate choices, so that freedoms, privileges, principles and obligations can be shaped in keeping with the supreme rule of circumstance, eagerly called the necessity for change. This is why preserving a civilization is of concern to moralists, builders and producers, while a society is dominated and run by scientists, psychologists and bureaucrats, often called managers or organizers.

I believe that civilization is more of a value than society, and that civilized man is a more complete human being than societal man. I also think that in a democratic organism freedom and capitalism are intertwined, and that a new relation between the free enterprise system and culture has to emerge to save the American civilization from a disastrous tyranny of culture gone astray.

A couple of years ago, anyone could have read a review of a play entitled *Flowers* in *The New Yorker* magazine, once a journal of moral taste and ironic sagacity, today an organ of penthouse radicals with six figure incomes and guerrilla bandanas over their face-lifts. It went this way:

> "—*Flowers* revels in vivid acts of masturbations, sodomy, cunnilingus, and fornication — and with violence only indirectly sexual, like murder by hanging, garroting, shooting, stabbing . . . [it] is an admirable embodiment of the homosexual transvestite's ideal of parody . . . [it] has the help of a company of six men and a woman, whose young bodies, often entirely naked, are lithe and well disciplined and a great pleasure to watch.—"

A pleasure to watch?

Is this already the decadence *a la Americaine*, the fall of the North Atlantic Rome amidst a jaded drivel? Is this stupidity or depravity or both? I think it is neither one. Even if in this case the theater critic was just another dull writer in pursuit of modish poses, a more complex and potent rot lurked behind. Namely irresponsibility consecrated as a liberating force. But the American civilization cannot be excepted from the rules that govern the history of civilizations. When cultural dehumanization becomes anointed as social and artistic value, when moral stupor is sanctified as the "new" aesthetics, tolerance and elegance, and is enshrined in the unholy edifices of fashionable cant, into which *The New Yorker* and suchlikes have become so helplessly remodeled — only an open rebellion against *this* culture can save us and the best in us.

CHAPTER 13

The Age of Information*

1

> "...Face it, punk sex is in...Purely animal-ethic has sunk into our consciousness... 'Let me tell ya what love is,' shrieks the lead screamer of the Dead Boys as he moves a vibrator up his inner thigh...Boudoir seductions are almost camp, whereas bathroom blow jobs are coming up fast..."

These lines are about teen-agers. They describe the punk rock scene, the new frontier of 14 to 17 year olds. They also give an insight into what may be going on in the nation's high school restrooms.

They come from a magazine which is called *High Times* and it peddles the use of lethal drugs from newsstands across America. Its ads inform about where to get marijuana and hashish and how to perish through them. It traffics in forged identity cards for teens. It propagandizes attitudes. The quote above is an agitprop piece, a slogan for 16-year-olds. It advances a fashion of stuporous fornication, of debasement as fun, of uprooting all feelings except the crudest biological spasms. A generation of humanoids emerges; they attain the nadir of existential experience at the age of 15, and, at that point, they have already transgressed everything for which a lifetime was once needed. The only option for thrills left to such dehumanized and defeminized amoebas will then be the thrill of destruction — be it of oneself or of others. Any moral consideration succumbs to atrophy.

Fashion is osmotic, it reaches an entire stratum and it somehow touches the immune as well as the susceptible, the depraved and the decent. Its influence is only a matter of degree, and *High Times* is massively read by youth. Which, to my mind, renders the First Amendment moot.

2

The current condition of American morals, manners and mores is caused by ideas. It is a trite assertion, but convoluted and murky as well. For example, the idea behind the First Amendment was noble and wise. However, even the wisest and noblest ideas become disfigured, life weathers them like it does the greatest and most durable edifices. Only when we steadfastly refuse to turn them into taboos can we preserve their propitious function and impact.

Nowadays, the First Amendment seems to be a most glorious law from

*A lecture presented at the U.S. Industrial Council's conference in Washington, D.C., October, 1977

which the spirit has evaporated. One has only to read a copy of *High Times* or *Hustler* to recognize this. No one mourns this attenuation more than I do: to me, whose faculty of expression was constantly massacred by various totalisms, the political sense of the First Amendment is one of mankind's paramount achievements. But the life seems to have gone out of the First Amendment together with its spirit. Every law is composed of both letter and spirit, and, I, for one, go with Bishop Berkeley toward preeminence of soul. I am thus scared of laws devoid of spirit. The spirit of the First Amendment was not and could not be a plea to protect the Flynts, *Hustler*, Hefners, Guicciones and *High Times*. In my view, their existence and prosperity in this democracy is a blatant travesty of the laws and of public sanity. So let's consider what has happened to an idea which crucially contributed to America's greatness.

It has fallen prey to the phenomenon of liberal culture.

Of course, the adjective "liberal" in that term has lost its ancestral exactitude, and it has come to signify a mood rather than a set of principles or ends. Anyone coming from Europe, who throughout his life had associated liberalism with Lockean Reason, Voltarian Tolerance and Actonian Liberty, quickly discovers its different face in America. Here and now, liberal has come to mean abandoning reason for wishful thinking, and tolerance for the bigoted novelties of half-baked scientism. When Jim Crow, human rights and errors of justice were still issues under debate, the liberal ideological excitability performed needed services. When it turned into sociopolitical programs, or began to shape the national culture, the liberal disposition obviously wreaked havoc.

3

How does the liberal culture manifest itself on the personal level since, during the last quarter of a century, it has reached an all but absolute sway over education, the mass media and entertainment?

When you find that, upon entering the teens, your child begins to speak a different language about elemental values which you have learned to cherish either through experience or diligent thinking — the liberal culture has entered your home.

When at your dinner table ideas and attitudes that seem to you both brainless and destructive are proclaimed but not discussed — you have gotten the liberal culture in your family where it subverts the notions of reciprocal esteem and turns relationships into role-playing.

When, after reading an article or a book, or watching a play or a movie that struck you as absurd, trivial, banal or grossly divorced from reality, you find in the papers and on television reviewers and critics lavishing praise and recognition (which is, of course, money) on what stands in contradiction to everything you know and believe in—this is the liberal culture promoting its cherished ideal — that of a cultural bazaar where nothing is weighed morally or rationally. A moral and rational appraisal of cultural facts is viewed as coercion by the liberal conscience; therefore, the scales in every booth are hopelessly rigged. In such a marketplace, as Saul Bellow once noted, everything is explained but nothing is understood. If, in addition to your astonishment that trash is hailed as revelation, and accordingly rewarded, you feel impotent to do anything to counteract the perversion of truth and value —you are accurately sensing the totalitarian element which pervades this allegedly free and democratic culture. So amidst the bounties of the liberal culture, you see your own helplessness, and you find yourself wondering what could possibly link this irrational tyranny with liberalism.

If there exists between a man and a woman something once called love, but the reality around gives the impression that words like *faithfulness, attachment, communication, devotion* have lost their sense — it is the liberal culture, which asks people to die for waters and plants, while, for inexplicable reasons is hell-bent on destroying the natural ecology of the sexes and generations. Other ancient words, you may notice, are also mysteriously missing from novels and songs. This concentrated assault on perennially cherished sentiments appears to be directed at *your* love, but in fact it threatens everybody, even those who lead the attack. If you have a strong suspicion that it is *not* equal pay for equal work that is actually being sought, but the idolatry of change for change's sake — you feel even more defenseless, because the liberal culture is attacking the substance of your existence and neither the system of checks and balances nor a Republican president can help you.

Finally, when the doleful outpouring of platitudes coming from your TV set offends your intelligence, yet is at the same time applauded by specious anchormen as matters of grave import — you feel a strange and shameful powerlessness. Your intellectual faculties reject the repulsive and paltry doctrines that are being thrust upon you in your own living room, but at the same time you know that active opposition is doomed to frustration. It is precisely at this point that you realize the totalitarian nature of the liberal culture. It is a totalitarianism which is deeply entrenched and so kinky and disguised that it can be sold daily to millions as the workings of American democracy.

4

To my mind, culture in our epoch has achieved definite hegemony over politics and economy, that is over those powers which in the past governed culture. This outcome cancels Marxism as an explanatory method. As usual this contradiction has taken place in America, a country which impudently has thwarted Marx's predictions on all counts. Recently, culture did away with a war that politics deemed necessary, and with a president whom it despised for aesthetic reasons.

Contemporary culture has brought into particular prominence a phenomenon in the arts and literature that has surfaced in the past, but never so blatantly as today. Art, drama, poetry has always had the power to embellish the ugly, the immoral, the sinful — even if the artist's intention was to accuse, decry or demolish. Shakespeare or Dostoyevsky had a unique power to so dramatize crime and guilt as to give them a didactic impact. The 20th century's prime art medium, the cinema, has turned this interrelation upside down. A century ago, only a few of those who read Baudelaire followed him into assorted vices. Establishing Lizzie Borden as a horror heroine didn't inspire a wave of crime. Somehow during our lifetime, Western man's ability to distinguish between good and bad has become hopelessly debilitated. Serious movie critics observed long ago that film is capable of making malefaction, wretchedness and abomination poisonously alluring. Even when the filmmaker intended to demounce, he often ended up with an image which attracted more than it repelled. With the arrival of television, the mass imitation of factionalized evil became a social issue.

I claim the title to a law that binds sociology with morality. Tyrmand's Law goes: "With technology's power to distribute culture, any wrongdoing that is not forthrightly labeled as evil and insistently condemned, will be recklessly promoted."

Let's explain what may sound obscure. If a murderer pictured in a movie is not unequivocally rejected as human scum by the script-writer, director and assorted critics, but, instead, is nurtured in psychoanalytic and sociological pseudorationalizations, his murderousness is promoted as a sort of contemporary virtue. His sins are wistfully exonerated by the repressions encountered in his unhappy childhood and the venality of the American system. A dopey slut from a feminist novel becomes a paradigm of sensitivity and independence. A massive youthful audience is out there, ready to stylize its aspirations on such pictured colorfulness. Punk rock is trampling the primary norms of civilized existence, but CBS News is eager to report its "vitality" and "message," while *Time* magazine raves about its musical depth. The lack of condemnation turns into instant promotion.

A question: why did the American press and media become the foot soldiers, even the elite corps, of the liberal culture?

The routine answers offered by paperback sociology stress that most students of the liberal arts and humanities who join the press tend toward the liberal persuasion; the other go into business, politics, etc. However, a great many of the active journalists in the various media swear to their nonliberal convictions, and most of the small-town newspapermen in the South and West openly affirm their conservatism. Contradictions aside, we all know that the liberal slant of the media is fact and truth. The American press and TV not uniformly but massively support the liberal causes. Not the political ones, as there is abundant evidence of press support for less than liberal candidates for office, or less than liberal political legislation. But this is the heart of the matter: the American press has given its unqualified support not to liberalism, but to the liberal culture, and these are not the same.

5

The liberal culture is the knight errant in search of oppression. The knight is far from lily-white. Thus, wherever oppression cannot be confirmed by reason and empiricism, the liberal culture fabricates it. The American press has long considered oppression news, which has assured many newsmen a place in the pantheon of American virtues. But lately, the liberal culture has come up with a wonderfully self-serving insinuation: that the press itself is a victim and in constant danger of unspecified repression. The First Amendment, they lament, is in the clutches of politicians, bigots and capitalists who will soon suffocate its usefulness to liberty. As proof, the Pentagon Papers, Watergate and the Larry Flynt affair are most often cited.

As an immigrant, I have tried to thoroughly understand my new country. I have never been free of two haunting quandaries: why do people in America get so excited about baseball and about the ridiculous notion that if we prohibit the publication of *Hustler*, a holocaust of civil rights will ensue? Why should squeezing out this festering boil signify an invitation to slavery? Why would it be a *precedent* — a word to which the liberal hysterics and histrionics attach a metaphysical function, a portent pregnant with the vilest consequences? In point of fact, it is hard to find in American legislative history an example of a precedent which led to the curtailment of freedom: consorships were installed during wars and unfailingly revoked, and we *are* actually engaged in a merciless war with greedy and heinous pornographers who strive to destroy precious and vital sensitivities. The LibCult's champions are unable to demonstrate how barring Flynt from selling women's debasement could limit former Senator McGovern's right to freely sing of his lust for Fidel Castro in public. After all, we have constructed a civilization in which we cannot even open a can of soup without faithfully following written instructions, that is precisely phrased law. The liberal culture's allegation that the American press is imperiled by an ever-impending proscription is a mystification founded on imputations and rather trivial mendacity.

Then why the liberal bias of the media, and what does it mean?

It means that the American media do not give a fair hearing to ideas. They propound, herald and disseminate liberal ideas, or, more precisely, the ideas of the liberal culture, while pulling down a curtain of silence on voices that propose others.

What in the realm of culture does the press defend today? What values did it defend during the 60's? It is easy to assert in an editorial that one is for freedom, equality and justice for everyone, but what about the *other* values by which many of us live and struggle? Can anyone recall any well-publicized case of a firm stand by the American press against the ludicrous abuses of good sense which devastated the American universities? Or against the promotion of moral callousness and behavioral idiocy in entertainment, so often attributed by the press to a capitalistic commercialization of culture, but which in fact is an offspring of the liberal culture? What has the press done to discourage the transformation of our youth into amoebas whose Weltan-schauung is based on the "poetry" of the Kiss rock group. Kiss, the punk rockers, or the Rolling Stones couldn't survive without the free but liberal American press. The media's overeager and gleeful support of abomination as pastime has become the cultural pus of the century, the moral gangrene of entire societies. A shattering illustration of this process is given in *High Times* in its October, 1977 issue:

> "...the media attention [was] leading to the mass turn-ons of the mid-Sixties..."

and further:

> "A wave of media publicity about the gentleness of this mass turn-on resulted in an even larger gathering in San Francisco's Golden Gate Park in January, 1967. An estimated 10,000 turned-on..."

What would an editor's response be to a charge that his paper is a functional accomplice in the destruction of American youth through narcotics? Most likely he would give the routine answer: "It's news and our duty is to report it. The grandeur of the American press rests upon reporting on everything." But where were the repudiations in editorials, condemnations in articles, any revealing of the repugnant nature of narcomania in features? Why didn't *Harper's* and *The New Yorker* for the sophisticated, and the tabloids for the common folk, berate this self-destruction with all the power the press commands? What's not condemned gets promoted.

American journalism has succumbed to the lure of the liberal culture. Instead of condemning evil, psychoanalytic quacks posing as thinkers, healers and social theorists enrich themselves by analyzing callow instincts and stylized poverty, and obtain nonstop exposure from the media. Human potential movements are assisted in hawking the snake oil of "self-improvement" whenever they contrive a new fraudulent prescription. The *New York Times* runs a story in its "Family/Style" section entitled "Jersey College Uses Pornography in a Sex Attitude Workshop," telling about a professor who has the earmarks of a latter-day Dr. Moreau. His obvious goal is to turn people into sexual protozoans and eliminate the last shred of intimacy from human sexuality. "All feelings and attitudes are good..." pontificates a Dr. Francoeur of Farleigh Dickinson University to the *Times* and that tower of liberal rectitude was happy to impart it to us "objectively." But try to find in the *Times* a report on psychologists and philosophers who claim that sexual moderation and privacy are good for your health, or that these modest virtues foster civic rectitude and make civilizations thrive.

6

There's a kind of contempt for both human rights and democratic fairness which I regard as overt totalitarianism of the press. Once newspapers reflected definite political colorings and diverse ideological opinions. Today, the big newspapers promise to mirror all shades of opinion. But is this pledge fulfilled? Big newspapers practice tokenism: we find columnists of opposing ideologies in their editorial pages, and the letters to the editor section is allegedly open to everybody. In fact, we all know that it is a manipulated fairness. The Op-Ed Pages supposedly offer an outlet for dissenting views, but it is dissent under rigid control; if the editors intensely dislike some views, those views will never see the light. And what the editors most dislike are not opposite views, but *intelligent* opposite views that make an irrefutable point.

To my mind nothing better epitomizes the cynicism of a paper which lays claim to moral standards than a story prominently featured in the *New York Times* during the 1970's: it was an interview with a pair of "darlings of the human potential movement," — a thoroughly repulsive couple of libcultural anthropologists who, some years before, had published a book entitled *Open Marriage* in which they advocated marital infidelity as a remedy to the ills of the era. The book received ecstatic publicity through the channels of the liberal culture, and the *Times* contributed mightily to its success. However, the authors now admit that their recipe for easy happiness failed, that many of those who tried it ruined their lives. The anthropological hustlers feel no remorse for such a trifle as a lost life; in their perception, it is not the rottenness of their theorizing but their victims' lack of sophistication which must be blamed. They informed the enchanted *New York Times* interviewer that their "truths" were for the elites, not the masses. But they did not mention that their work was designed for the unsophisticated to make it sell, and not for the scarce consumers of "Satyricon" or Crébillon-fils. Never mind that such classic representatives of the raffish breed of pseudoscholarly mountebanks were the natural progeny of the liberal culture and were thriving under the umbrella of its social morality. The question remains why the *Times* once again advertised them in an interview filled with catchy platitudes and phrased with sympathetic quasiobjectivity, thereby compounding the original offense. What is not condemned is automatically promoted, and whatever the detachment of tone, with this interview the venerable *Times* promoted the patterns of promiscuity, pernicious to many existences, merely by focusing attention on the modish intellectual swindle.

Why is it so? Where does this all-engulfing tidal wave of liberal destructiveness and corruption originate if the people who constitute the American press are not all blindly committed liberals?

Focusing upon one national newspaper and analyzing its contemporary ideological structure may provide an answer. Let's look at the *Chicago Tribune*, a weighty and influential journal. During Colonel McCormick's tenure it was a paper of a strong Tory commitment, perhaps not always on the enlightened side. In 1969, a change occurred, extolled in *Newsweek* as "vaulting the *Trib* into the 20th century," and a subtle but insidious mechanism was put into action. Reading the *Tribune's* news and editorials, one acquires a sense of impartiality, middle-of-the-road politics, a moderate approach to the national issues and local problems. The philosophy of mild Republicanism is felt: labor is admonished, the business community cautiously supported, Cuba disliked, Angola mourned, judges are censured for leniency. But just look into the cultural sections and the picture changes dramatically, multicoloration turns into a pervasive pink hue, occasionally into outright red. The book section features some reviews which would easily be accepted by Moscow's *Pravda*. A reviewer of the Jessica Mitford's disgusting memoirs wrote: "The mean and sinister are those who sought to persecute and prosecute communists in the belief that they were dangerous..." These are words printed by a "responsible" American newspaper at a time when people already know how *dangerous* the communists were to those 20,000,000 murdered Russians, to Budapest, and Prague, and to every American attempt to protect rationality and good will in the post-World War II era. Reading this sentence one hears a protracted groan from Colonel McCormick's grave, a wistful lament that fellow-travellers are in business on Michigan Avenue. The "Lifestyles" section ran a story on Angela Davis and Jane Fonda, and called them "a silent force for good." A protesting letter sent to the editor on this subject was not printed. Instead, it was privately answered by the editor's assistant. The same would happen to someone who wrote a letter to *Izviestia* or *Literaturnya Gazieta*: their response would not be different in tone and effect than that of the *Chicago Tribune*. This is why it is no mistake to call the *Chicago Tribune* a liberal totalitarian newspaper. Oxymoron is the liberal culture's natural law.

7

The liberals have made culture their vehicle and weapon. They sensed the future accurately and cultural endeavors became, quite early, the engines of their current triumph. It is enough, today, that the zealots of the liberal culture control those media departments which diffuse culture, and those which are supposed to express the public opinion at large — like the letters to the editor section. Republicans and nonliberals own the *Chicago Tribune* and even express themselves in its editorials. Libcultists use it to fetter the minds, penchants, sympathies, lifestyles, even existences. Is it possible that the journal's leaders have not noticed this state of things? My guess is that they intentionally support the pseudoenlightened moral relativism that makes some capitalists such difficult allies in the struggle for the survival of capitalism. Cultural fashions are as hot a merchandise as *haute couture*, and too many capitalists do not ask questions about the intrinsic value of what sells well.

But out there, there are millions of people waiting for someone who will tell them how to cope with that tremendous power to distort, slander and annihilate almost everything they believe in, cherish and live by. People are waiting for someone to tell them how to dispel the pornographic pollution without abolishing free enterprise; how to destroy the booby traps of permissiveness without stifling personal liberties; how to improve our social system without having the libcultural sophistry and charlatanry impose upon us make-believe solutions. There are people out there who yearn to know how to mete out justice to those who trample on it. And above all, people crave to be told how to be human and humanitarian and still preserve solid authorities, moral traditions, community cohesiveness and economic efficiency.

La lutte finale for humanity and Americanism will take place on the battlefields of culture. Thus, the order of the day is to defend culture from the liberal conceptualists. The Founding Fathers, whom both liberals and nonliberals claim as their own, spoke little, if at all, about social paternalism and the liberation of instincts as the road to social order. They spoke about Reason, Responsibility, Morality, Humane Ends and Values. In spite of its touted allegiance to these words, for the liberal culture these are odious euphemisms of oppression.

CHAPTER **14**

The Innocent and Unhappy American*

These days, the innocent American is unhappy. One may ask: Who cares? The answer is: Everybody. The world learned that it has a vested interest in America's happiness. When America is happy, the world-at-large, whether it is down on its luck or just cynically greedy, gets a bigger share of free food and only slightly-used clothes. Even those who openly curse the same America which provided them with the bread they couldn't cull from their own soil — tilled with political slogans and fertilized with the blood of murdered peasants.

Of course, there is no automatic connection between innocence and happiness, and guilty but happy people abound. But American innocence has always been a source of strength, energy, activism and diligence. A decade ago, I went to the U.S. to immerse myself in this innocence. When asked about my nationality, I used to answer: "A U.S. immigrant." To me it meant a merger with something I had always admired. To many I appeared disgusting and pitiable. "What's so great about living in this country?" was their routine reaction. The time was the '60s and the liberals had nonnegotiably declared America a plastic and immoral desert. They had pronounced the melting pot a failure. They demanded courses in colloquial Swahili at Harvard. They wanted the Puerto Rican kids to learn Spanish in primary schools, while all the kids wanted was to watch *Gunsmoke* in official English. But from my first glimpse I noticed astute Irish politicians, honest Italian cops, clever Polish businessmen and martinetish Jewish admirals — all contradictions in terms. To my mind, the melting pot brewed the strangely alchemic, great American innocence more efficiently than ever. A disturbing feature of this innocence was that all one had to do was to climb a soap box and shout: "Freedom good! Oppression bad!" to have healthy looking adolescents repeat in a trance: "Gee! What a revelation! No one else has ever thought of that!" Snake-oil, America's most potent potion, was being bottled by the liberal culture.

Something much weightier than political passions were in the making. It looked like American culture had been invaded by some shady powers. At the beginning of the '60s, the American culture was a rich amalgam, but its shapes, colors and flavors were still distinct. The overall success of this blend was overwhelming, some called it cultural imperialism. America needed no propaganda, jazz and blue jeans did the job; denim became the only unstylized folk attire in history which was transformed into urban elegance. Hollywood gave world-wide popularity to the uniquely American notion that decency could be an attractive source of modish poses: Humphrey Bogart in *Casa-*

*From an address delivered at the Aims for Freedom and Enterprise Conference, London, England, July, 1978

blanca projected a corny sentimentality that was the epitome of chic. Whether Hollywood marketed didacticism for money is irrelevant: this didacticism wrought one of the healthiest civilizational climates known to mankind.

The '60s marked the watershed. American culture came under lethal attack by forces which had hated it for decades. The assault was aimed at the juncture between innocence, youth and normalcy — a devilishly chosen spot. Oscar Wilde wrote: "The youth of America is its oldest tradition: it has been going on now for 300 years." Reducing youth, innocence and the sense of normalcy to one giant pulp of mass idiocy was the decisive point scored by those who were after power. When it comes to the exploration of the interplay between a new, albeit pernicious, idea and its social ripple, no one can beat America.

Those shady powers have long understood that Marx erred when he assigned culture only a tertiary role after economy and politics. Besides, he picked the wrong class to determine mankind's fate. The proletariat might have had a moral claim to this role, but would have remained helpless forever without men of thought. Men of thought, from the Pharaoh's Egypt on, served everybody. Not long before Marx, they helped the bourgeois producers to knock out the well-born sybarites. Soon thereafter, they decided that the middle-class capitalism that had given them limitless freedom and financial security didn't satisfy their yearnings for power, and they declared it both immoral and hideous. They realized, sometime in this century, that the worker could be subdued as easily as the bourgeois destroyed. In 1917 they initiated a society in which idealistic economists and angelic bureaucrats were supposed to supplant grasping capitalists and provide people with food, clothing and shelter. The results are well-known. What they learned from this experience is that people can be loved but never trusted with freedom. The militant post-Marxism of the '60s and '70s gives ample proof of these feelings.

Then came the mass culture, mass communication and the mega-university, and the intelligentsia concluded that it didn't have to share its power with anyone. It created its own ethos and philosophy, developed a social infrastructure called bureaucracy, and reinvented absolutism as ideology. It then discovered the socioeconomic synergy of the ultimate cultural weapon — the communication medium, printed and electronic press — and ruthlessly proceeded to monopolize it, make it an intelligentsia weapon, which gave it an unheard of power and control over society. Unlike the ideologies of previous class sovereigns, which had been derived from religious devotions, patriotic sentiments, or humane propensities, the contemporary intelligentsia, the everlasting producer of kinkiness, has grounded its ideology in sublimations, perversities and libidos. This is why the totalitarian tendencies of its *Weltanschauung* are called liberalism in America.

The liberals in America decided to deprive the middle class of its ethical values and economic well-being. To a liberal, traditional American ideals are the cradle of vile intentions and moral corruption, American folk culture a pathology, business spirit an evil, America's military and economic potential the chief threat to the world. Curiously enough, the liberal nominates himself as the American civilization's staunchest defender. His loudest castigations are, of course, anachronisms, as we no longer live in the America of Lincoln, Twain, Rockefeller, Mencken or General MacArthur, that is in the America of Republican humanism tainted by snobbery and money. We live in the post-Kennedy America of George McGovern, Ralph Nader, radical chic, Bob Dylan, affirmative action, Larry Flynt, Jimmy Carter and vaginal art — a liberal America which the liberals have conceived, determined and fashioned via the *New York Times*, NBC, *Time*, and *Ms. Magazine*. It is *their* America which they inexplicably disapprove of, whose culture they incessantly mold, and, in the same breath, accuse of bottomless depravity and vulgarity.

The liberal intelligentsia's most coveted virtues are elasticity of mind, and change as a value in itself, regardless of its results. Semantics is its pastime, like the medieval nobility's tournaments. They have invented their own double-think and newspeak. Paradox is its political weapon, hypocrisy a skill. It calls its ideology liberalism — a shameful abuse, because true liberalism, a rational persuasion, was structured from the sense of freedom's responsibilities. Liberal moral passion, or sense of duty, has become the totalism of the intelligentsia.

In the '40s, a distinguished educator, Gordon Keith Chalmers defined American liberalism as "the smoke of unexamined feelings." It soon evolved into a hierarchy of prejudices. In the '60s, the liberal intelligentsia succeeded in creating a climate of fateful incoherence. The media moguls, Hollywood chieftans, the satraps of the bureaucratic-educational complex are the manipulators of imagination: even if they do not run the country, they run its daily life, through TV, the record industry and heat-transfer printed T-shirts. They have made both politics and the economy their solicitous sycophants. Their *modus operandi* relies on an advanced cultural weapon system. For instance: synergism. An example: Mr. Rupert Murdoch, a Commonwealth import, a multimillionaire and press monarch, operates three publications in New York. In the *Village Voice* he relentlessly promotes the most vicious kind of social hatred. In *New York Magazine*, he encourages moral atrophy and the anarchy of conducts. In the *New York Post* he supports politicians and ideologists who meretriciously declare themselves on the side of social hatred and anarchy of conducts. The synergistic effect of such influences becomes a formidable power. One may ask: What proof do I have for ascribing to Mr. Murdoch such black-hearted villainy? Not much more than the force of reason. The media in America claim that they only reflect reality. This is the Big Lie of the century. The media *create* reality in America, and therefore constitute the most effective device to rule the society by an autocratic establishment of which Mr. Murdoch is a prominent member.

The ideological fuel was provided for the Murdochs by the class ethos of the intelligentsia. In the '60s, the liberal theorists chose normalcy and common sense as the targets for their warfare. For over a decade, intellectual concepts have radiated from the educational and creative centers only to be simplified by the journalistic footsoldiers and TV entertainers, and dispatched with a frighteningly energetic frequency of pressures. One may ask: Isn't this an attempt to demonize the role, the intentions, and the purposefulness of the intelligentsia? Aren't some members of this class the staunchest opponents of liberalism, followers of religions, dedicated conservatives? Certainly, as in all human affairs, there are no neatly stacked absolutes. But we live in an epoch of the power of cultural thrills. The old hedonism of enjoying life only through refinement and plenty is passé. Transcending, even violating, normalcy has become the new hedonism, controlling images a quest for significance. Today, perhaps, one third of Chicago's population can dine, at least a couple of times per year, at *Le Perroquet,* and occasionally indulge in buying luggage from Gucci, or a Calvin Klein ready-to-wear dress. Two thirds can find deceptive imitations at Montgomery Ward. Being elected to political or municipal office today is mostly a matter of competitiveness in America, not an automatic ascension to power. But forming images, manipulating beliefs, implanting modes of thinking in the mass mind guarantees an endless place in the spotlights, write-ups in the press, a position in the opinion-making process — now the only sovereignty among the powerful.

The results are disintegration of the social fabric, the extermination of standards, the specious operations performed upon the human mind, the fostering of social and individual anomalies, the disruption of interhuman rapports, the vandalism of sexual norms. Literature can no longer be dirty, it has to be unwashed. No society in history could ever endure *a la longue* this state of affairs. Even Will Durant, one of the most venerated liberal thinkers, expressed alarm by saying: "I believe that life depends upon an adjustment of order and liberty . . . Any emphasis on one or the other is destructive." He is echoed by a prominent liberal, a Harvard professor of government, Michael Walzer, who wrote not long ago in *The New Republic:* "Morality rests most deeply on a series of prohibitions: *Thou shalt not . . ."* And this is the heart of the matter. Permissiveness — the liberal intellectual and moral style — is in lethal conflict with common sense. Prohibition — the liberal notion of a social plague — is in full accord with the human sense of normalcy. Common sense and normalcy are the two red buttons which start most crucial confrontations between *Weltanschauungs* in today's America. The presence or absence of common sense is the pivotal point of the clash. Common sense is an organic element of existence. It resists fallacious egalitarianism, denies that standards of living can be raised by guaranteeing a minimum wage that nobody is going to pay. Capitalism is a manifestation of common sense. Nothing brings into focus the liberal hatred and scorn more than does common sense and those who are committed to it.

Nothing, that is, with the exception of the notion of normalcy. Normalcy is a civilizational bond. We have to feel bound by a norm to live a meaningful life. A liberal, even believing in law and morality, accepts normlessness;

normalcy these days spells repression for him. For us normalcy is the cornerstone of civilization. We do not feel repressed by a norm, but by its absence. It constitutes our best appeal to people who do not understand us too well. I, for one, firmly believe in: "Right or wrong — my civilization!" Paradoxically, it is an elitist motto in the era of feminist aberrations, Elton John's "poetry," and sex-shops for truck drivers. But: "Right or wrong — my normalcy!" is an easy way to communicate with a large number of good people in an age when politics begins at the family dinner table and in the neighborhood movie house, when sexual distinctions have fallen into the hands of a sinister cabal of ideologists who are trying to use the wide horizons of the American Constitution to rewrite the human constitution. My slogan makes a lot of sense in the struggle against TV's intent to fetter the society's consciousness, as we become what we see, and what we see is horrendous.

There is still hope in America that innocence, as much as it has been battered, can be transmuted into a new serviceable image. Some of its characteristics may be irrevocably gone, but some of its essence may survive. Those who call themselves conservatives in this cognitive mish-mash, do not believe that it was better before than now. They believe that once certain ideas were conceived that have never lost their validity. They do not want to preserve old arrangements, but old values by which people tried to live, even if they failed to live up to their promises. They have never claimed old medicines were better, but old wisdom might have been. They wish to shape the future in accordance with ideas which have never been proven wrong, only declared wrong. Today, if one voices cultural beliefs which are also conservative, one is denied recognition as a good writer, reliable scientist, or honest politician. Hamilton and Madison were the last conservatives who were culturally and intellectually accepted and respected. In Europe, political or financial power has always flirted with intellectualism and arts, creating the deep and rich culture of conservatism. In nineteenth century America, money and political power scorned intellect and culture — and we are now paying dearly for this narrow-mindedness. It has resulted in a kind of transvestite capitalism that subverts itself in various business enterprises, and is evident among certain politicians who walk into the arena calling themselves conservatives, but lacking any understanding of conservative cultural roots, perform as clowns.

Today civilizations, societies, wars, economic systems, presidents and politics are at the mercy of culture and its approval. Culture should have a free interplay of ideas, but all ideas are not equal or equally valuable. The French-Romanian philosopher Michel Cioran said: "A philosophical fashion catches on like a gastronomical fashion: one can no more refute an idea than a sauce." It is the faculty of the human brain and the power of humanity to select and choose between ideas, and to discriminate between right and wrong ones. Freedom cannot be divorced from authority and responsibility — and to believe so is enough, in the liberal culture of today's America, to be accused of un-American activities. But there is hope in America for a restored humanism of normalcy and common sense. As for me, I cannot find a better example of what I see as hope than this classified ad from a "Personal Column" of a not-too-reputable magazine:

> "*Pro-Capitalism*
> Single w/m, 43, seeks romantic relationship with a not-overweight young woman who is procapitalism, proreason, anti-God. In your reply please name your favorite author."

Everything in the microcosm of one human being's priorities, desires and preferences — culture and conservatism, common sense and normalcy, innocence and incoherence — is in these two sentences. Apparently, in today's America we are doomed to dealing with the entire package.

CHAPTER 15

Drugs & Fashionable Nihilism*

In 1928, Sarah Martin, a now-forgotten black singer, recorded a blues with King Oliver. She sang:

"You made me roll and tumble, oh, Lord . . .

You made me weep and sigh . . .

Made me use cocaine, but you wouldn't let me die . . ."

These lyrics specify cocaine as an agent of human suffering, defeat and degradation. The drug is recognized here as both an existential scourge and a symbol of ultimate downfall and disgrace. Death is mentioned as a more *desirable* option than dependence on narcotics.

In 1980, a promotional ad for *High Times* — a publication openly committed to the support of drug use — reads:

"The magazine of getting high is now the magazine of feeling good."

In its pages, *High Times* fondly calls cocaine a "recreational drug." Its editors and writers do not overtly recommend sniffing, but they seem determined to create a mood of cultural and behavioral preferences — supported by a plethora of deliberately misinformative data — which will persuade their readers to do exactly that.

The promotional punch line consists of code words which sound laid back, low-key and cheerful, drenched in stylish informality. In point of fact, they constitute a credo of ultimate and sacrosanct weightiness. They encompass the quasi-religious core, metaphysics, ethics and mystique of the ideology of fashionable nihilism. "Getting high" stands for a dope-induced stupor and the debilitation of human faculties. "Feeling good" is fashionable nihilism's First Commandment, a rigid instruction to what must be worshiped. Together these phrases form an emphatic directive for how to live. Every line of *High Times'* propaganda is thereby altered: it cannot be perceived just as an invitation or encouragement to use drugs; it assumes the prerogative of a commander of minds whose awesome power rests upon fashion and modishness — formidable and terrifying weapons in a free and permissive society. Getting high and feeling good become the only ontological and moral obligations of a human who has been blueprinted by *High Times*; its editorial henchmen have thereby embarked on a crusade whose goal is to make society operate on their principles. We may suspect that Sarah Martin, certainly not a

*Presented at an International Symposium "Drug Abuse in the Modern World", College of Physicians and Surgeons of Columbia University, June 20-21, 1980.

squeamish bluenose, would be astonished to know that cocaine — her wicked oppressor, tormentor, the source of her calamitous agonies — is now, fifty years later, proclaimed as a prime ingredient of well-being. She would proba- bly find it impossible to understand that drug abuse is no longer considered, at best, an illusory relief, but — conversely — a symbol of sociopsychological health, serenity of interhuman rapport and moral perfection. It would be beyond her grasp that the breezy, ostentatiously relaxed advertising slogan lifts drug addiction to the triple role of progress, social truth and human worth. Finally, even if "feeling good" beclouds the mind with bestiality, it nevertheless is touted as enlightenment, and every release of impulse comes to be extolled as a higher state of consciousness. At this point, we can best see how fashionable nihilism's perverse dialectics so easily translate into a profit- able commodity. Its easy-going casualness, its popular off-handedness and its hip explicability through colloquial obscenities all create a market for vendi- bles which can be pushed not like forbidden fruit but like food and shelter. In such a sociocultural climate, the financial powers that be, from the Mafia to the honorable banks with branches in Turkey and Colombia, can feel absolved from any sin. The dispensation comes daily from the honorable members of academia, more-or-less honorable authors and authorities pub- lished by honorable Manhattan houses, and from honorable press organs which do all they can to avoid any judgment or any mobilization of public opinion against the time bomb planted by *High Times* and its accomplices in America. A well-oiled conspiracy of silence enables *High Times*, and with it the entire drug subculture, to thrive. In keeping with basic rationality, the vicious purpose of the *High Times* theorists should be openly and frontally attacked by Congress, the White House, universities and the journalistic towers of rectitude like the *New York Times* and *CBS News*. However, nobody does it. A notion prevails that if the situation is ignored it will fade away, like other subcultural bad smells and bad habits. But *High Times'* gangrene and pus will not disappear by blinking at them, only by squeezing and cutting them out.

Why is it that, during the last half-century, Sarah Martin's grief has become laughable in the eyes of *High Times'* operators and afficionados?

My answer is: because a sunny-side-up concept of narcotic hallucination as part of the human and social reality has evolved and has been declared to be a civil right. A large segment of the American intelligentsia has proclaimed the freedom of narcotic experience as an ideological tenet. We know *how* this came about; my generation witnessed it firsthand. Yet, if we wish to avoid simplisms, it is difficult to deliver a satisfactory and comprehensive answer to the questions of *why* it happened, *which* are the philosophical, social and cultural vectors that produced the victory of such a concept, and *why* the society failed to develop a stronger antitoxin than law enforcement to thwart the influence of an ideology so obviously destructive. To my mind, two factors can be named: the liberal culture and the pernicious self-serving character of the modern, omnipotent media. In our time those factors have come to connote a combination of attitudes made possible by the bizarre alliance between intellectually self-seeking academia and trashy pop culture.

Sometime during the mid-60s *Sturm and Drang* of the liberal culture, drugs emerged as a powerful coefficient of the sense and flavor of the epoch. I do not intend to retell the old story: we all know that chemical hallucinogens became the incense and myrrh of the times, that the marijuana code of honor, together with blue-denim mysticism, found its way into *Vogue* magazine and the cultural power structure. Smart-alecky journalists began to speak about the Drug Culture as a part of the *Zeitgeist*, random crime in the streets skyrocketed, American inner cities turned into jungles of fantasmagoric cruelty, radical proselytizers warbled on TV talk shows about the collapse of our civilization. They never attributed this collapse to the use of drugs, but always to American imperialism and the oppressiveness of American institutions which drove sensitive people to escape reality.

If — during mankind's history — transcendentalists and mystics ever ascribed any propitiousness or beneficiality to stimulants (other than purely spiritual or psychological ones), they all, from Aztec priests to Swedenborg to Hermann Hesse and Aldous Huxley, insisted on endowing such experiences with extraordinary gravity and status. The theorists of a human id standardized by the so-called counterculture of the 60's proclaimed the ingestion of cocaine to be about as important as a bicycle ride or a checkers game, a pastime, an exercise of one's nervous system, an endocrinological frolic, the pranks of imagination that go so well with gourmet cooking and the pleasures of sailing. The expansion of consciousness through narcotic experimentation was defined as the rediscovery of functional bliss, of innocent naturalness that had been eradicated by the bourgeois culture. From here, it was only a small step to announce that narcotic intoxication constituted a higher degree of humanness and, consequently, a vehicle to mankind's perfectability, a final *passe-partout* to holism and millenarian utopia. Pot became gnosis, its wholesale application was supposed to improve the world, tame evil and elevate mankind to a state of grace. In other words: the use of drugs ultimately came to mean a moral virtue and existential value. However, during the 70's the popular mood drifted away from the sacrifice, loftiness and anti-imperialist martyrdom of suburbia. This is why *High Times* speaks these days of just "feeling good"—a winsomely blithe, chirrupy and modestly subdued phrase.

This, certainly is a novelty, the most "in" and "new" variety of nihilism. The previous prophets of fashionable nihilism, from Petronius to de Sade to Max Stirner to the French *décadents*, unanimously subscribed to the momentousness of drug addiction, to the morbid glory of their self-destructiveness. *Apres nous le deluge* was their battle cry, and they would fiercely defend their right to lofty courage, pathos, the sinister extraordinariness of their exploits. They fled the reality they shared with others not just for "fun" but in order to emphasize their high-powered hatred and contempt for the conventional.

They *knew* the consequences of drugs and they *wanted* them to be devastating so they would make a proper impression on their enemies, the bourgeois conventionalists. Baudelaire cared very much about an appropriate setting of haughty tragicality for his sinfulness: this is why he preferred *le mal* as the designation of his propensities—he would furiously reject the invitation to "feeling good"; he would fight to the end for the "beauty of corruption," for the dignity of his pessimism and catastrophism.

The smirky, arrogant flippancy of pro-drug attitudes began some time ago with Genet, William Burroughs and Allen Ginsburg, and it leads straight to *High Time's* hit squad. The rock subculture helped a lot. A fateful socioeconomic aberration of our civilization makes it routine for four or five protozoans with amplified guitars to spout a message of mental retardant in front of enormous audiences and be paid fortunes for what amounts to trickling poison into defenseless ears. Their financial rewards alone are monstrous and pathological and bode ill for our chances of suvival as *homo sapiens*. Their hammering propaganda for drugs is unrestrained by any rational or moral factor; actually, their cognitive apparatus is unqualified to encompass the drug phenomenon either generally or as a particular instance in life — Pavlovian acceptance is their only proposition. As such, their influence upon youthful psychologies far exceed any other cultural aggregate — school, church, parental guidance, intellectual stimuli — and something is terribly wrong.

The traditional cultural aggregate has fallen victim to the pressure of the liberal culture's notion that not perdition but idealism, gentleness, avoidance of wronging oneself and one another is the ultimate consequence of drugs. No one bothers to explain how this version of vice transmogrified into virtue meshes with the reality of dope-related violence. Which brings us to the malfeasance of the press — perhaps the most blameworthy component of our predicament. To the overwhelmingly liberal American press, the drug problem is one of individual freedom: it cannot be curtailed under any circumstances. The press are thus defending their concept of an absolutized First Amendment — the paradoxical source of the media's unlimited, totalitarian power within the American democratic universe. What the press try to avoid is their responsibility for moral action. The *Times, Post, Tribune, Time* magazine, CBS, etc. will all eagerly publish information on the lethalness of addiction under the motto of "the people's right to know," projecting themselves as humble servants of "the people." However, reporting nothing more than the findings of doctors and scientists, and examples of drug-related debasement and heinousness, is a hypocritical cop-out. The school of thinking that assumes that facts of a horrendous nature are a deterrent is doomed in advance: in our technotronic reality, as molded by the omnipotence of the media, even law becomes an illusion, the victim of endless relativities. Drug abuse is a moral and cultural problem and it's exactly on moral grounds that

American press refuse to confront this problem, claiming value-neutrality as their badge of honor. Individual freedom, whose champion the press pretend to be, is inconceivable without individual obligation, self-control, discipline of mind and heart. The moral acceptance of drugs does not mean free will at work: in fact, it means coercion of fashion, submission to lifestyles and cultural ambiences which are generated by the media at large. Thus, the worst enemy in this war is *not* the conceptualist, the theorist, the ideologue, *but* the popularizer — and *those* who report *without* denouncing, popularize. The contemporary culture, with its monumental pervasiveness via TV, movies, records, etc., beautifies anything it touches, even when it means to repel. Whatever monstrosity is depicted in a Manson or Reverend Jones story, its rendition in the media attracts imitators; in the business of modern distribution of cultural images and symbols, what's uncondemned is promoted. Thus, in the struggle against disintegration, the free American press, as mighty as it certainly is, is not the ally of the people. It would be futile to expect moral support for the antidrug cause from the press, or to expect it to acknowledge its uninvolvement and bogus impartiality. In its quest for dominance in America, the liberal press has as much to gain from the forces of fashionable nihilism as from those of rationality.

Does this attitude of the establishment press make for an objective support of fashionable nihilism and *High Times's* abject subversion? William Burroughs, no mean authority, once wrote:

"Junk is the ultimate merchandise. The junk merchant does not sell his product to the consumer — he sells the consumer to the product. He never improves his merchandise, he degrades the client."

These words acquire a peculiar significance when we become aware of the scary might of the American media, which was founded on the ruthless pursuit of the ultimate merchandise that would make it possible to sell the consumer to the product. And when we realize that commercial TV never improves its merchandise, but constantly degrades the client, an uncanny parallel of purpose, or affinity of means, seems to loom between the junk merchant and America's liberal mass media.

CHAPTER 16

Modern Culture and the Norms for Intimate Relationships*

The title above would please an ironist. It clearly pre-supposes that our moment in history still encompasses intimate relationships, taking for granted that these words have retained the meaning and correlation which my generation remembers from life and literature.

But is that the case? Here is one of those counseling services from the comic strip and horoscope pages in every provincial newspaper:

"Dear Dr. ...: I am 61 and had a heart attack a year ago. Since then I have not had an erection...I know some men who are older and who still have intercourse. Why can't I?"

The doctor-columnist is a serious professional; he thus delivers a long comment that ends on an up-beat note:

"If you are able to climb a flight of stairs without difficulty, you should be able to withstand the exertions involved in ordinary sex."

A belief that climbing stairs equals sexual exertion is a bit disconcerting. In fact, it's a back-up detail for a threatening phenomenon. The episode is far from "ordinary," as it is to the syndicated medical authority; such erotic zeal, undaunted by age and infirmity, seems quite imposing, Moreover, what counts is that here we are at the very center of the sense of norm of the modern culture—and the doctor meekly conforms to the reigning standard as he answers with the routine clichés of the human potential jargon. What could be more intimate than one man's relationship with himself? It is hard to imagine, but whatever it is, the most personal matter has effortlessly become a mass communication item.

Let's measure the man and his sorrow against larger criteria. His query epitomizes what the modern age has done to the concept of norm.

What's a norm?

Forsaking epistemology, we can say that a norm was one of the greatest inventions of civilization. For millennia, it served to coordinate human nature

---

*A version of this essay was offered as a lecture at the Rockford College Institute's seminar on the family in June, 1979.

with human concepts of how to live in and develop a society. It was best codified by the Judeo-Christian and Hellenic theology and ethics. Prior to the current reality, which has invaded us quite suddenly, the most commonly accepted norms were evident as the inclination to be ashamed of, or, at least, discreet about one's deficiencies, an imperative to control a vile temper, a tendency to conceal it if one happened to be a nymphomaniac. We are now witnessing the all-out disintegration of norms, as well as some grandiose attempts to replace them with something — no one knows what.

In the cited case, the customary norm has been replaced by what the modern prophets call entitlement. It is a new model of interaction between man and society, coined in the intellectual workshops of the liberal culture. It can be termed a key word to our epoch. Theoretically, it means that civilization and democracy thrive where people want, demand and obtain what they themselves think they are entitled to — regardless of fact, logic or objectivity. Their act of claiming is a precondition for their freedom, energy, prosperity, health. The gentleman with the lost carnal delights is already a creation of the modern culture whose gospel is daily transmitted to him by the media. He probably did not hesitate for a moment to bring his intimate affliction to public attention. We can surmise that reading about his own imperfection in the morning paper made him flush with pride: after all, both his physiology and his jauntiness receive an instant celebrity status, widely noticed and perhaps discussed. Modern culture, through all its modes of communication, has imbued him with a firm conviction that he's entitled to any form of sexual excitement regardless of birthdate and other prerequisites. Erection is his constitutional appanage, like voting. The sexual performance seems to him his social promise, owed to him by science, the government, affirmative action, the consumer movement, Blue Cross, Social Security. In a reality where narcotic hallucination and mechanical orgasm are seen by many as civil right, possibly to be warranted by some statutory law, he justly feels victimized when not getting his share. Who's to blame for such a deprivation? The columnist-doctor mentions natural exhaustion, or improper drugs, but more sophisticated theorists of entitlement know better. It's capitalism, the Puritan work ethic, the Congress, the American system of oppression and exploitation which are the real culprits of his failure. He's often told in the press that, actually, his feelings of being wronged are the most desirable and dignified norm of contemporary life in America. The doctor he addresses his grievance to, although he could answer him through private mail, chooses instead to publicize him, thereby contributing to the pollution of the public mind. The doctor, of course, believes in the liberal gospel of the paramount good of the publicness of desires.

Is the feeling of entitlement really a supreme norm of thought and conduct? If so, it is certainly at the expense of those norms of existence which establish the notion of normalcy according to reason and Judeo-Christian morality. Normalcy, that is the convergence of norms with our knowledge about ourselves in both spiritual and physical dimension, still remains, and probably always will, the most powerful conditioner of human existence. A diminished sexual potency at a certain age is normal. But the modern culture isolate the man in question from the sense of normalcy. Once this would have made him pathetic, even farcical. Today — it makes him and his inquiry a formidable cultural factor, if not a social power.

As culture always reflects civilization, their contemporary interplay bring us to another quandary. To my mind, the history of civilization is not so much that of weapons, tools and forms of organization, as that of the evolution of sensibilities. It began with the caveman's realization that pain might be felt not by him alone, but also by someone whom he happened to be clubbing to death; in other words: civilization began with the recognition of the sensitivity of the other person.

Consequently, culture began with the fig leaf, that is by introducing the first norm of behavior and feeling about the particulars of our being. Whatever the explanation as to why it happened that way, whether it is provided by the Good Book or Darwin, gnostic philosophies or dialectical materialism — the rationality of this orderly sequence of the development of norms is our clear civilizational profit. Culture is mostly about what happens between man and God, man and himself, man and woman, man and another man. If civilization is about bringing humans into community through likeness and mutual bonds, culture is about differences and compromises, obstacles and reconciliations, nagging questions and impossible answers, comfort and discomfort of emotions. If civilization is about being and knowing, culture is about what we *want* to be and what we *wish* to know. To move through its black holes without a norm is like traveling through cosmic space in Bermuda shorts. It would be perhaps too broad a generalization to assert that the dissolution of all civilizational norms is already an everyday feature; after all, we still find parking tickets on our windshields. However, the decomposition of norms for intimate relationships is exactly what modern culture is all about.

More than any other, Western man is structured on a public-private dichotomy. This has to do with the history of Western personalism and individualism and sets us quite apart from other societal traditions. Everyone, from medieval heretics to Lenin, who has tried to change this separation of personal things and public things by dint of a new doctrine, has been doomed to defeat.

For millennia, intimate and sexual relationships have been a point of contention: They belonged to the realm of the private. However, both religion and state have had a long history of trying to extend their normative influence from mere interpreters of the laws of God and society to that of legislators of feelings and destinies. Not too successfully, to be sure, which, consequently, after many bitter struggles, brought about a specific truce between church, state and human sexuality, and ever since has become a trademark of Western humanism — both religious and secular. Judaism and Christianity deftly recognized those zones of subtle imponderables that define the psychosomatic creature — King David, St. Augustine and later Pascal had many wise things to say on this matter. We all agree now that the Hester Prynne ordeal in *The Scarlet Letter* was a most unfortunate affair, and people who respect religion and its interventions into things human should always find it deplorable. Even if subject to countless cultural fluctuations and variations of time and changing moods, the norms for intimacy have been deeply, even eschatologically, grounded in the sense of privacy. Though there are no proofs that the strategists of the modern assault on norm were out to upset the balance between the private and public realm, that is exactly what they seem to have achieved. They have done it through culture, not by doctrine; they have destroyed the vital dichotomy of public and private by means of fake recipes for newness and progress. The assorted "liberations" have trampled with cowboy boots all over the network of norms for intimate feelings so delicate that even the bigots of the past did not dream of tampering with them. Those feelings once belonged to the individual person; often to one's family; depending on one's faith — to the confessional; and on occasions - to one's doctor. They are now public property, candor about them today is seen as a social virtue. The human being, as defined by classic humanness, has fallen prey to advertisement: it all began with the uninhibited-by-any-norm mass publicity for deodorants and laxatives and ended with reducing the sexual universe to paperback "how-to" manuals. Secular utopian movements, like feminism, invaded the world of the interdependencies of men and women. Secular utopianism has played a crucial role in the annihilation of norms: whatever its thrust, women's liberation or egalitarianism, it often scores spurious successes which attract attention and bring easy acclaim. It spectacularly influences the marginal paraphernalia of life but never its fundamental variables. The feudal serf never dreamed of asking for cost-of-living compensation; his unionized descendants do — and they get it. However, secular utopianism is, by definition, destined never to realize its most solemn promise, one that constitutes its spiritual and moral propellant: whatever its reformist or revolutionary accomplishments, it cannot succeed in eradicating the feeling of disillusionment, inadequacy, injustice, purposelessness, bitterness and dissatisfaction with one's self. It can never satisfy the eternal human craving for more than can be had. Feminism is archetypal in this respect: it promises to alter the unalterable but it settles for novelty and superficial appearances of change. What the secular utopians hate most is the mercy of an established norm.

The ultimate ruin of the public-private dichotomy is best exemplified by another letter to the all-too-humane doctor mentioned before. A thirteen-year-old girl complains about a missed menstruation and dramatically inquires whether she is pregnant in spite of the fact that she is a certified virgin. The doctor uses the opportunity to deliver a sex education lecture about the menstrual irregularities among "young women." Young women? The correspondent is self-admittedly a thirteen-year-old, but this instant upgrading is necessary in the crusade against the norm and the liberal doctor has no qualms about treating her as an adult; he is not above the sleazy craving for sensationalism. How many primordial norms are violated in this one case? Does the girl's anguish, if it is sincere, belong to the public? Isn't there an ominous moral trend in this blatant exhibitionism? The popular culture finds various ways to verbalize human tribulations. In the '50s, Billie Holiday sang a song about the miseries and cruelties of life with a recurrent line: "Ain't nobody's business what I do..." It might have sounded rebellious or anarchic then, but it suddenly acquires a sense of individualistic responsibility when cast against the normative slogans of recent decades like "Let it all hang out!" or "Open up!" There is a palpable emotional and moral difference between "anything goes," which absolves the "Me Generation" from all obligations, or "Do your own thing," which is an apotheosis of cheap egotism, and "Nobody's business by mine," which means, first and foremost, a readiness to accept consequences, a personal accountability to sin, error and woe. Terence's famed *Humani nil a me alienum* has been variously interpreted: Emerson translated it, "I'm a man and nothing human if foreign to me," and saw in it man's inability to escape misfortune and grief; Anatole France inclined to see in it a pivotal absolution for human foibles, failings and vices. In fact, "Nothing human is alien to me," and all the moral ramification of this simple fact, is a superbly formulated norm of our being. The modern wreckers of the norm submit this normative wisdom to a strange transmutation and declare: "Nothing that's mine should be alien to others." Such an inversion of truth and values opens the floodgate for an avalanche of social triteness, which makes thirteen-year-old girls discuss their most intimate properties of soul and body in the daily press, and eagerly publicize them with the help of allegedly conscience-oriented doctors. The most bizarre aspect of this interchange is that both the girl and the doctor may think they are alerting or sensitizing the general consciousness. Actually, they are hopelessly benumbing it.

It is possible to trace the roots of the now-obvious disintegration of norm as a category of living? Let me try to do it in a simplified survey of some very complex matters. Sometime during the eighteenth century, novelists began to notice that it is *not* only fate, history, society, character and emotions that shape the human psyche, but also the existence of another human which forms human beings. Later Stendhal, Dostoyevski, Proust and Joyce brough this observation to full bloom; Freud theorized and codified it in the language of science, and the belief that man is another man's most potent formative factor became the focus of Western Culture. But none of them has ever ignored the preponderance of normative morality. Freud, who had a genius for naming and describing the phenomena of inner life which had always been known to mankind, firmly believed that no psychological problem could be solved except in the context of moral principle; his successors were to destroy such principle by equating it with social condition. But then came Albert Camus with his conclusion: in his novel *The Stranger*, a man kills another man for his mere presence, with no other reason than that he *is* there. We were made aware that modern life has shattered fundamental norms and modern culture is helpless to do anything about it, other than to register the fact.

Another subversion of norm has its source in the romantic tradition of spontaneity of feelings that, in its ultimate consequence, superimposes *lack* of moral or rational order over *any* order. Romanticism, that powerful nine-teenth century movement of ideas credited with great progress of man's mind and soul, found its final expression in the so-called counterculture of the '60's, whose gist was the triumph, beatification and enshrinement of immaturity at the expense of maturity. As immaturity means the cult of amorphous, instinc-tual and inchoate — the victim became norms of regulatory elements of life and the world.

The terminal blow to norm as a guide within the universe of human intimacies came with the modern version of sexuality. Until now, when two persons entered a sexual relationship, the widely acknowledged norm of belief and feeling was that *something* had happened between them. For three decades, the modern liberal culture has assiduously toiled through all its channels — education, mass-culture, pop-art and entertainment — to implant the notion that a sexual encounter has no meaning and nothing actually happens except for some physiological sensations. In the past, two persons used to perceive a sexual experience, even a fleeting one, as a bond, even a most tenuous one; as a certain mutual presence in one another's life, or, at least, a certain knowledge of one another. Only whoredom, a term encom-passing more than its explicit meaning, was bondless, free from any intimate obligation, thus paying the ugly price of alienation and depersonalization for this freedom. Now the depersonalization of the act has become its value; the disregard for bonds, mutual knowledge, and all reciprocal rights is the new virtue. The sexual act has turned into a nicety, a minor favor granted for nothing, like an act of politeness in a crowded subway. It has been reduced to a grimace, and the theorists of this development — in medicine, psychology and *Playboy's* offices — tell us that we are liberated because we can make faces without inhibition, immaturity's ideal. This reduction of humanness — our civilization's substance — is crucial to the understanding of our age. When morality becomes almost exclusively a social notion, norms become obsolete. When ethics become a function of social relations, their relevance to human intimacy ends, and only social acts qualify for moral evaluation. The norm begins to escape us, it becomes nebulous in relation to a relationship, a nuisance when linked to anything intimate.

The suspicion that marriage may not be the best arrangement between two specimens of opposite genders is an ancient one. However, this nagging sentiment has never been a threat to the institution itself. Marriage seems to be like democracy, of which Churchill said that it wasn't a very good political system, but is better than any other we know. This is a tricky observation: the ills of democracy, so crass, obvious, seemingly easy to condemn and to heal, go deep into the abyss of philosophy, where nothing is simple. We know about the dangers of mobocracy and the terror of the vulgar; yet, we know too, that liberty and prosperity thrive where the rational and responsible one-man-one-vote system is widely respected. The human desire for a meaningful bond — seen by some as bondage — is perhaps what makes both marriage and democracy indestructible fixtures, sources of difficult virtues, to which we always return after binges of experimentation.

Is marriage still the norm of commitment in the modern liberal culture? Merle Haggard and Leona Williams, archetypal country-western signers, singing about their budding love, epitomize the contemporary foul-up of notions with a refrain: "We oughta be together..." One would assume that, being spokespersons for the Southern lower-middle class love ritual, they should know something about marriage, choice, family, formalized together-ness. But they are already welded to CB radio courtship manners, victims of the patterns for life advocated by TV talk shows broadcast from Manhattan or Burbank, on which dull-witted sociologists and psychoanalytical entrepre-neurs tell them how to live. They want to express the natural yearning for association, but they have lost their sense for the naturalness of norm, so they flounder around, groping for meaning and articulateness. The time-honored prescription for solidifying a relationship has been eaten away by *Hustler* magazine on roadside diner counters.

Marriage is no stranger to enraged assaults which unite against it the most unexpected partners. A couple of years ago, a San Francisco hooker attemp-ted to organize prostitutes and housewives into one labor union, and the liberal press went into raptures over her proposal. She drafted a feminist *Women's Declaration of Independence* and announced in the name of the liberation movement that: "Wives perform the same jobs prostitutes do — although most wives don't do them as well because of lack of practice and training," She was, of course, unaware that the spiritual fathers of the liberal culture have been saying the same thing for a century, and G.B. Shaw even wrote a play about it. The idea is not so new as it seems to be, and it's a sort of miracle that, in spite of the century-long dissection and denunciation of marriage, the wedding ring industry still survives. "The lesson all women learn: men are the ultimate enemy..." declared Marilyn French, the ultimate feminist-intellectual oracle. But marriage is a durable norm and apparently it's not that easy to eradicate it from the human vision of existence. We all know that "they lived happily ever after" is a preposterous lie, but we also know that slightly amended as "they had their ups and downs, but, on the whole, they lived quite happily together," is something that we all would regard as a blessed and gratifying sense of normalcy.

Which brings us to family as another cherished norm. Somewhere is his *Institutes of the Christian Religion*, John Calvin called those who violated parental authority monsters, and demanded that they be put to death for disobedience. His method seems a bit exaggerated to us, but — notice that this kind of rigidity looks different if one is wholly committed to the family as a norm of goodness. Moreover, love — not a value to be dismissed lightly — has constituted the supreme norm of family life for millennia. Family as a fundamental cell of civilization was an attempt to structure authority upon love and as such, it failed as frequently as it succeeded. The proposition of accepting emotional obligations in order to achieve emotional fulfillment will always beckon; thus, any trend to dissolve the family in order to eliminate its torments appears to be doomed to defeat. Even if it sounds paradoxical, the family is the bastion of freedom and provides the pleasures of civility — whatever constrictions its detractors see in it. Professor Christopher Lasch, a liberal *sans reproche*, wrote in *The Culture of Narcissism*, a celebrated work: "The medical and psychiatric assault on the family as a technologically backward center...went hand in hand with the advertising industry's drive to convince people that store-bought goods are superior to homemade goods..." and he goes on to berate educators, social-welfare bureaucrats and therapists. But things are not that simple. Throughout history, there have been various concepts of family: feudal (a source of power), clannish (source of pride and fighting spirit), economic (a source of productivity), religious (a source of transcendental values), teleological (an answer to mortality and transience), cultural (a source of determinants that shape a person for life). Then Freud came along and said that family feelings mold the human being so forcefully that they do not always contribute to happiness, well-being or psychical health. This now seems to be a platitude; in his time it was a discovery. But Freud was also wary and distrustful of the word "liberation," claiming that he had no idea what it should mean; Milton was his beloved poet. He correctly pointed out that ethics, not research, should define human conduct. He failed to announce unequivocally that the family is a positive norm in itself; that civility, compassion, forbearance, countless feelings and attitudes, can be institutionalized and bureaucratized by state, church, science and social organization, but only the family can personalize and humanize them. Family does it through a unique ambivalence of sounds, smells and tastes; only the family successfully blends censure with approval, rejection with love. Only the family has the instinctive capacity to deal effectively with disruptive interactions. Unfortunately, Freud's brilliance turned into appallingly small change in the hands of his followers: they proved unsurpassed in turning utter banality into alleged wisdom, thereby committing cultural crimes of yet unassessed dimension.

No one can tell now whether our sense of norms and of intimacy has been terminally damaged. In an era when the wives of presidents and statesmen are warmly cheered in family fournals for "kicking a habit," that is when sleaziness of character is regarded as just a complexion problem, gloom is inevitable. The havoc wrought upon norms and intimacy by feminism — whose essence is an abyssmal jumble of misconstrued freedom, equality and justice, but whose faithfuls believe that they are creating a better world — the ravages from this source are indescribable. Ivan Turgenev, the great Russian novelist, wrote around 1860 (that is over a century before ERA became an issue): "To tell the *true* story about a drunken *muzhik* beating his wife is incomparably harder than to compose a whole tract about the woman question..." Insight like this somehow alleviates our pessimism. We cannot comprehend why the liberal culture pushes bestiality as the mainstay of its art; we know that mankind, at its early stage, has gone through reveling in cruelty as entertainment. Then, a long process of refinement followed, and only with great effort we have learned not to consider abomination a pleasure. Refinement primarily involves the norm of sensibility, the attachment to what is humane, civilized, even if skeptical, to what I'm fond of calling moral elegance. Thus, I'm the first to admit confusion when I read the morning paper about the Harris Poll findings under a heading: "Family, peace of mind first for Americans; sex, money, love last!" This, beyond any doubt, is a poignant public outcry for the reestablishment of norm. But is a surge of simple human decency and uprightness enough to effectively counteract the perniciousness of what the coalition of zealots and operators imposes upon us as a better world and modern culture? I don't know, especially when I read the following:

"Attendance at the Anglican church of St. Michael's and All Angels doubled Sunday following charges that the new vicar had seduced the wife of a former parishioner. The Rev. Ralph Thicknesse, 57, was accused by the husband of a woman in the vicar's previous parish of carrying on an affair with his wife. However, many worshipers backed their new priest. One woman said, 'We will forgive him for whatever he has done. He seems to be a very nice, friendly man.' "

CHAPTER 17

Notes on How to Live*

"It was a long, long time ago, perhaps last Friday..." Winnie-the-Pooh used to say. Some forty years ago (which to history is only last Friday) a jazz singer by the name of Lee Wiley sang a blues entitled "Down to Steamboat Tennessee." It went:

They say a times a comin' when a woman won't need a man

They say a times a comin' when a woman won't need a man

I'm gonna keep that time from comin' if I can...

I'm afraid that today these lines would be regarded by feminists and many others as an outrage, a call to oppression, a calamity. Yet they contain one of the preconditions of human nature; the correctness of Lee Wiley's choice can be rejected only at the cost of the most nourishing instincts that have preserved the species on this planet.

Thus, why is it that something which affirms the rudiments of existence in the lyrics of a song that portrays us as we truly are is considered by so many people to be inimical, invidious, corrupted?

Most likely the reason is that the ideas which engineered the contemporary culture have passed a verdict that determines how we should live. In this particular instance, we are confronted with an idea which assumes that a woman does not necessarily need a man to fulfill her destiny as a woman. The consequences of this idea are multiple: among other things, it has — to a large extent — restructured the patterns of how we already live.

In the journalistic din of our days, when reporters spout psycho-analytical lingo with the agility of a hot-dog-stand operator, we constantly run into feature articles which inform us that the rate of divorce quadrupled during the 60's, or that the number of unmarried couples living together tripled between 1970 and 1980. Reading these articles, I get an eerie feeling — as if a silent-movie slapstick tempo had been applied to the statistics: they suggest that until the 1960's people divorced at a relaxed pace, but once the calendar turned over to the 60's, suddenly Americans began feverishly to divorce, or shack up, with the speed of an animated cartoon. The question that comes to a developed mind is: Why? Why would a society that divorced seldom in December, 1959 start to divorce hectically in January, 1960? What could be the reason for such an acceleration? Neither *Time* nor *Newsweek* bother with such questions in their smart-alecky reporting on what they call social change:

*Printed in: Imprimis, March 1982. Presented at Hillsdale College, MI, November 10, 1981.

all they want is to inform about the change and to quote from books which claim to describe it. Professor Jacques Barzun, the eminent educator, wrote: "Thirty-six years have passed...(since the publication of his renowned work *Teacher in America*). The once proud and efficient public school system of the United States has turned into a wasteland where violence and vice share the time with ignorance and idleness..." Again, anyone with intelligence would ask: "Why? Isn't it possible to point out the culprits who are guilty of ravaging an institution that served us so well for so long?" However, neither the *Washington Post* nor any other self-appointed conscience would venture too deeply into such an investigation; it might show that Professor Barzun's 36 years are about equal to the length of the hegemony of liberal thought in education, that those 36 years coincide with the publication of books that recklessly promulgated ill-advised ideas for change, ideas whose aim was to "bring education closer to the people" — a spurious claim, since American education has always been of and for the people. What happened during that time was that two generations of liberal prophets declared personal integrity, responsibility and self-reliance to be dubious qualities, tools of corporate capitalism's mental repression, devised to keep Americans locked into apathy and subservience. Since then, rebellion against any established order has been saluted as a supreme virtue; self-reliance was denounced as naiveté and moral responsibility as superstition. Now, in the 1980's, that Professor Barzun's wasteland has been realized, the liberal media — perhaps the most insidious culprit of the current educational quagmire — who, for 36 years have hidden from the public any but liberal concepts of education, suddenly unleash their propagandists to tell Americans that *they* have invented the idea of teaching honesty, responsibility and self-reliance. In other words, the media seem to be rooting for another change — without acknowledging that the conservative critics of previous changes were right.

Of course, first come the books and then the change. The all-encompassing answer to "why" there have been so many divorces and such a collapse of education is culture, but the mass media are reluctant to admit that the ideas promoted by books of *their* culture for years have been inculcating behavioral habits into people's minds, foolish novelties about and modish attitudes toward marriage, divorce, fidelity, marital obligations, personal propensities and penchants. The media scarcely wish to confess that those ideas have finally resulted in the splitting of families and in a surge of various forms of what, not long ago, would have been called living in sin or trampling conventions. The media won't ever admit that a cultural model, derived from a body of ideas, quite often tells people how to live by means of sleazy gossip columns. A *Chicago Tribune* columnist recently wrote that the messy dissolution of norms we are experiencing today is the work of two men — Elvis Presley and Hugh Hefner. He credited those two subhumans with the transformation of the nation's mores to a greater extent than any philosopher or statesman was ever able to accomplish. He was not entirely wrong, only depressingly shallow. Presley and Hefner would never have bloomed if certain cultural formations which were rooted in ideas had not *allowed* them to flourish, if those ideas had not consecrated and endorsed their subcultural products. The nihilism, born of philosophies and novels of which they had never heard, long preceded Presley and Hefner.

We *all* live according to culture. What is culture? There are countless definitions; I, for one, subscribe to one by a Polish writer of my generation who died young, but first wrote: "Civilization is fork, spoon and knife. Culture is how to use them."

About civilization, Orwell said that it is all of us. His is a definition poignant in its directness. The key word to Western civilization is quality. In no other civilization has quality — that is the excellence of efforts and results, be they spiritual or material — been declared of such paramount value as in the Judeo-Christian one. Quality also means honesty of endeavors and a supreme concern for intellectual honor, a concern that cannot be dismissed by cynicism, or fatalism, or man's cosmic frailty. The Western notion of quality assured us of prominence in the world, but for the last half-century we have failed properly to translate that notion of quality into culture, that is into patterns for what to believe in and how to live. We have lost the qualitative meaning of life. The loss of the sense of quality, out of which the Judeo-Christian concepts of reason, personal responsibility and social freedom have structured Western civilization, has become — to my mind — the crucial issue at this juncture of American history.

Is this failure the result of some inherent defectiveness in our civilization, or it is a disaster we have brought upon ourselves? I tend to think it is the latter. I also suspect that what nowadays is contemptuously called the bourgeois culture was infinitely superior to what is currently imposed upon us as cultural values, tenets and *Zeitgeist*. The bourgeois culture's quest for quality — be it in social arrangements, personal relationships, industrial products, economic ethics or the texture of daily life — was not without deficiencies, hypocrisies and abuses of conscience. Yet, since the twilight of the bourgeois culture during the 1920's, since its practical abolition in the 1960's, no subsequent proposition has even approached the stability and psychomoral orderliness of the bourgeois culture, with its ability to create prosperity, foster progress and produce lasting values — from the bourgeois social contract to bourgeois cuisine. Never in history has a culture been more hospitable and beneficial to art than the bourgeois culture: it simultaneously served the artist as a political protector, an economic supporter and a benevolent target of art's most vicious attacks. The more an artist hacked away at the fabric and texture of bourgeois morality the more highly rewarded he was. We finally reached the stage of the "liberation" subculture of our time, where the postbourgeois society pays rock stars astronomic payments for its own demise, and artistic rebellion means clownish assaults on constrictions that no longer exist. The bygone nobleness of the bourgeois culture was at the core of its own debacle: its own righteousness begot modern American liberalism which, in turn, refashioned the notion of liberty into a value vacuum. Sometime around the beginning of our century, philosophers began to intimate that valuelessness is the true measure of freedom. In Europe the void was soon filled by Marxian and anarchist, then fascist and Hitlerian prescriptions for deliverance. We now witness a dangerously analogous process here, chiefly among the strata of the American intelligentsia. Its cultural compass and agenda, as they were formed in the 20's and peaked in our time, were never to understand man — the sacrosanct principle of the Judeo-Christian civilization — but to explain him. We are now in the midst of an age of dumbfounded discoveries of everything we have known since time immemorial. History, philosophy, sociology, psychology, the entire field of humanities, which, for millennia, dealt with the exegesis of man as a bearer of values and creativities, became mere sets of instructions, like those that are routinely enclosed with a factory-boxed bicycle. The endless explanation of how to assemble man and humanity to make them operate according to the instructions of Marx, Lenin or just Masters & Johnson became a cultural commandment, a promise for secular salvation. Our cities are permeated by evil, embodied in the beastly juvenile who takes life at random, but ours is an epoch when those who still insist on speaking of evil are called simpletons. Those who deny the possibility of man's wickedness and savagery are hailed as sages. The foolish benignity with which those sages teach us that evil is as curable as acne is called scholarship and decency in the newspapers. All of which pushes us closer and closer to the catastrophe of cultural idiocy sanctified as supreme cultural wisdom.

Sanctified by whom?

By those who rule our culture, continuously turning it into the liberal culture. Let us not make a common mistake: liberalism and the liberal culture and *not* the same. The former is a philosophy which teaches that our goal should be a society that's both free and fair — a respectable end toward which the liberals have strived through rather ill-conceived means. The liberal culture is what liberalism has done to culture, especially to the American culture — that is, to a body of beliefs, traditions, customs and attitudes which are preserved in morals, manners, notions of value and decency and their artistic rendition. The relation between liberalism and the liberal culture is similar to the circumstance where handsome, estimable parents produce an offspring who is a genetic monster which, in spite of its gruesomeness, must be loved and defended.

How do we measure the liberal culture's directives and manifestations against the Judeo-Christian and American heritage, against the notions of human dignity, reason, normalcy and common sense — with which that culture now appears to be waging a merciless war? The answers may be found in seemingly disjointed metaphors.

In *Ms.* magazine, a certain Elizabeth Janeway, feminist theorist and intellectual beacon of women's "liberation," cannot bring herself to a clear-cut censure of incest; she wavers in her judgment. She implies that incest may be a matter of negotiation between people who shape the predominant cultural pattern according to which the rest of us live. It means nothing to Ms. Janeway that the authors of the Bible, Sophocles and Dr. Freud saw incest as the ultimate disintegration of humanness. Ms. Janeway agrees that it may be a misdeed, perhaps indecent, but her reasoning is drawn from anthropology rather than ethical emotions. She is unconcerned with how incest kills man's inner sanctum, how it robs human beings of the spirituality of passions, how, to many, it is the terminal expiration of sensitivities. Ms. Janeway's lukewarm anxieties are not about our sense of normalcy — a primordial issue in a decaying society — but about "patriarchal myths" or about whether the participants in an incestuous relation experience "negative or positive reactions." Her premise is that "contemporary commitment to personal freedom invites us to challenge old taboos as being obsolete." She asks: "Are there limits to liberation?...We still face some uncertainties..." The title of her article, "Incest: A Rational Look at the Oldest Taboo," implies that she argues in the name of rationality. But to me, and to many like me, incest is the very heart of the human soul's darkness, and the manipulative psychosocial rationalism à la Ms. Janeway is an insult to my faith in reason and perhaps not only mine but also John Locke's and Voltaire's and Jefferson's and John Stuart Mill's, whose credentials in defining rational liberty are certainly not inferior to those of *Ms.* magazine; they never divorced man's spiritual, civic and political rights from natural law and normative ethics.

Yet when it comes to shaping obligatory cultural proclivities and popular tastes, Ms. Janeway's ideas will be seeping into the American collective consciousness and my ideological tenets will not. Most New York publishers and editors will print her views and refuse to print mine. Neither cultural nor intellectual freedom exists in today's America: they are brutally suppressed by the tyranny of cultural and intellectual fashion. Some will say, "nonsense" —anyone in this country has the right to speak out, to say what he thinks is true. That is correct. But not everyone has the right to be heard. The *New York Times*, ABC and the president of Yale University ensure that only those who voice ideas deemed proper by the liberal culture's establishment are heard and registered in the popular mind of this land. Ms. Janeway is a part of the reigning culture, and I am not. *She* thus determines American desires, ways of life and mores by means of culture; she, and others like her, dictate how Americans should live, even though she legitimizes the sin of incest by detaching it from mankind's everlasting certitude. What she and her co-ideologists won't ever realize is the ugly, destructive power of their pseudo-objectivism and quasi-rationality which is unanchored by any moral norm. She's unaware of the dominant culture's unholy might to promote anything that is not damned, to produce countless Jack Abbotts, and the narcotic mass suicide of our youth by cool, value-free reporting about them, by a presentation of just facts disconnected from any moral or empirical context.

She won't ever pay heed to mankind's eternal sureness that incest annihilates what should be inviolable, by murdering the notion of normalcy in us. Her rejection of unambiguousness is in fact promotion, for any modern mass diffusion of images and ideas results in *promoting anything*, even evil, if it is not explicitly denounced as evil.

This circumstance is even clearer in the quandary of a noted American socialist, Mr. Michael Harrington, who, in a recently published book (*The Next America*), wonders whether Dr. Martin Luther King, Jr. and "the rest of us" who called for violation of "unjust laws in the name of true legality" ended up with the sociomoral message that "no laws are binding." "Was our higher justice an incentive to common crime?", Mr. Harrington asks himself. But he is easily assuaged: a researcher on the subject of teen-age crime assures Mr. Harrington that the worst juvenile black felons are unaware of either the civil-rights movement or Dr. King's existence. And here is the very center of the phenomenon which predicates the liberal culture's power to form its how-to-live directives, its blithe nefariousness in imbuing those models with an apostolic innocence that so easily turns into existential evil. It is not what they preach — the Harringtons, the Janeways — but the cultural and moral climate they create that allows animalistic incentives to blossom, turning the contemporary scene into a jungle of senseless tragedies, whitewashed vice, emotional misery, psychological squalor, mental squalidness. The murderous black teen-ager needs to know nothing of Dr. King other than the fact that the late leader declared justice tantamount to retribution - because such distortion is, in point of fact, what the Black Panthers, the New Left, the Berkeley Free Speech Movement, the so-called counterculture, the rock subculture, assorted journals of opinion like *The Nation* and *Mother Jones* and, last but not least, their avid supporters in the *New York Review of Books*, CBS and *Playboy* have made of Dr. King's communication to American blacks. In a 1971 story about a black laborer in Detroit (who, in a fit of rage, killed three innocent people) *Time* magazine sounded somehow sympathetic to the killer - hardly Dr. King's vision of affirmative action.

This is where the silliness of the *Chicago Tribune* columnist comes in: he does not understand that Presley and Hefner are just sleazy artifacts of an idea for how to live, not its originators. They are the end products of John Dewey's and William James's thought and Edna St. Vincent Millay's poetry, of Thorstein Veblen's sociology, Charles Beard's history and Lincoln Steffen's social criticism—the respectability of those names and their endeavors notwithstanding.

About the middle of the 60's, America, and the world, witnessed the emergence of what I call the Behavioral Left — a sinister and far-reaching phenomenon which — contrary to Marxian prophecy — used the social elites as a weapon for an amorphous and sterile social change. This occurrence brought neither justice nor welfare to the masses; those elites were just armored vehicles in the all-out war against the Judeo-Christian philosophical legacy. It was sort of an ideological vampirism, a "Body Snatchers" toxic principle: anyone bitten or pollinated was henceforth a carrier of the disease. The final result was the breakdown of a civilization which had been erected on a special American mixture of 17th-century religious moralism revived by the 19th century's great sociomoral battles, together with 18th- century rationalism, which provided the legal and political structure of the American statehood. That glorious amalgam of reason blended with idealism and of moral concerns permeated by pragmatic principle made America great, the object of the world's envy, admiration and hope, the paradigm of practical democracy. Then, during our lifetime, American liberalism transmogrified into the liberal culture, and what we now see around us is a new America, a nation that is hostage to new prejudices, orthodoxies and charlatanries. The Behavioral Left is one of them, a direct descendent of the liberal culture; its battle cry for "emancipation of penchants," whatever their nature, has more in common with Hitler's *Blut und Boden* (blood and soil) ideal of prefabricated impulses than with what Aquinas, Pascal and Hume taught about man's inner resources.

The American democracy was, from its inception, rooted in the concept of social contract, in which prohibitions were carefully balanced against permissions. The liberal culture canceled that balance: instead, it introduced the limitless expansion of so-called human rights — to the point that the notion of rights became decomposed and its atrophy opened the door to a lawlessness that turned most of the social bonds into caricatures. Certainly human and civil rights can and should be rationally enlarged, but there is danger of human dignity's being mercilessly trampled in a process in which rights become, by principle, unconstrained by duties. There exists a complex interrelationship between human dignity, decency and unbound freedom, and these three categories were juggled much too nonchalantly by the liberal manifestoes of the last half-century. The most precious part of what the Founding Fathers devised for us *culturally* was that skepticism might not be enough to structure and institutionalize a decent and dignified freedom, but faith alone may not be sufficient either to build the City on the Hill. What enriches us is to be found between reason and faith; that golden mean has eluded men for millennia, but we Americans came closer than any nation on earth to crystallizing this ingredient as a propitious component of our society and our lives. That is, we were adamant in our slow pursuit of that ideal — until the liberal culture established its despotic reign during the 1960's. The bequest of the 1960's and the degeneration of the civilization prototype we inherited from the Founding Fathers can perhaps be best encapsulated in the recent exclamation of a 22-year-old president of student government at the University of Massachusetts. "Our human rights are at stake here!", shouted the young man during a violent protest against the school administration's decision to ban coed bathrooms in dormitories and the common use of facilities by both sexes. The postulate of unisexual body ablutions has thus become a sublime measure of fundamental freedom in the mind of an educated person. We can only guess the expression on the faces of Tom Paine or James Madison if they were told that, by the end of the 20th century in America, the supreme criterion of human rights would be an option of where, and in whose company, a bowel movement can be the most satisfying procedure. Here we can witness the impact on one feeble mind of the cultural climate in which grandiose goals are pursued by means of oppressive imbecility. Many of us feel that the world has become too small and too crowded for such a ludicrous distortion of common sense, but many who think that are unaware of the attractiveness of simplism, vulgarity and triteness — the best fertilizers on which the Behavioral Left breeds feminism and Red Brigades, sexual deviations and debased schemes of pleasure, abomination as entertainment and vileness as beauty. The abhorrent visage of The Rolling Stones's Keith Richards on the cover of *Rolling Stone* magazine is repellent not just because it is the physiognomy of a demented Dickensian highwayman, but also because it is imposed upon our reality as the aesthetics for our time, an exemplar of masculine charm, handsomeness and winsomeness once associated with human faces like those of Clark Gable or Gary Cooper. The Behavioral Left's only ideological vector is to destroy the old order, but as the moral order known to mankind prior to the 1960's is already in a shambles, its fury and venom actually have no outlet. There's nothing left for it except bloody terrorism or degenerate indulgence in repulsive grotesqueness of fun, the worship of decadent abnormality, obscene wealth, specious mysticism, debilitating sybaritism, self-destruction through costly narcotics — which ultimately means that the Behavioral Left has climbed into bed with all the moral enemies that it allegedly went to war against in the first place. Nowhere is this abysmal fraud more visible than in the current literature that is ceaselessly boosted by national magazines as our title to cultural glory. The mystifications of the Mailers, Vonneguts, Vidals, Updikes, Hellers, Doctorows, etc, are inherent in their literary premise, oddly common to all of them: that simplification and shallowness are immanent in our reality, that man's redemption is contingent on his commitment to sordidness, that his passions can be reduced to only violence, and that his freakish deformations are his beauty. No one has dissected this aberration promoted as refinement bettter than Saul Bellow in *Mr. Sammler's Planet*, an analysis of how psychoanalysis and liberalism rob modern man of self-respect, how the superficially enlightened and primitively satiated man becomes the doleful prey of alienation touted as higher consciousness, how lofty platitudes burglarize the individual and social ethos by preventing man from making honorable use of his own part in the spectacle of living. Reading Bellow, one realizes how the cheap modern psychologism cancels out all the literary components of the great fiction spawned by the bourgeois culture. "By their fruits ye shall know them..." sounds in the Behavioral Left's parlance like an advertisement for a homosexual hangout — and that may be the most concise statement of its impact on American everydayness.

Humans can be created or produced. History, religion, tradition, the family have all had the power to create people. Society can only produce them. Over the last 50 years in America, producing people became the ideal of liberal ideologues. The result is a tremendous number of children who are disconnected from any communication with parents, of people who have been so brainwashed that they can no longer understand words like "virtue," "civility," "normalcy," who are isolated from religion and deracinated from history. They became products of mores devised by paltry TV "sociology"; their brains were softened to the condition of rancid mush by moronic pop songs; they became commodities put together by scoundrelish mass-cultural operators, humanoids animated by a music inspired by man's never-extirpated inclination to brutishness. One Mr. Jason Epstein — shining light of the *New York Review of Books*, the announcements of which are the holy writ for the liberal establishment — recently blamed the all-engulfing picture of debasement, callosity and chaos on "the democratization of extravagance that has put us in this mess..." He meant economic rather than our cultural limbo, but his elegant ennui, camouflaging a trace of panic, can serve as an accurate pointer. All I need is to provide exemplifications of Mr. Epstein's *mot juste.* Our reality, recorded every day in the papers, teems with things which once would have been deemed insane, horrendous, nauseating or just shocking, but their nonstop reappearance in our awareness, even in plain sight, has made them commonplace. Perhaps the most cardinal sin of the contemporary culture is its ruthless extermination of the charm of the uncommon, the exceptional, the stupendous; when specialness turns into banality, *anything* can be endlessly trivialized, made the butt of callow jokes, become a matter of cursory practices. This is what has happened to sex education as both an educational idea and a social factor. By annihilating the notion of normalcy, we abrogated our sense of the extraordinary: our sanity is thus anesthetized — and this does not bode well for our survival as a civilization. What do we do when we learn that in some junior high schools in Humboldt County, California (reported by *The Public Interest*, Spring 1979), radical teachers teach — yes, teach — seventh graders how to masturbate, and Planned Parenthood outlines courses in copulation of seventh- and eighth-grade students? What we do about the practice of rock bands on the road, whose members assemble in their Holiday Inn rooms large numbers of 14-year-old girls and perform nude before them, endowing them with hysterias, torpors and psychological malfunctions for the rest of their lives? The Rolling Stones seem to be the masters of this cute leisure pastime, according to a chintzy journalist who writes their paean in *New York* magazine; he emphasizes how The Rolling Stones are *above* the law by dint of their genius and what a "massive, untapped" sociocultural power they are—which in the end means that they have a super franchise for telling people how to live. The idea of animated dildoes, which is all the existence of The Rolling Stones amounts to, has already made two generations pay enormous sums of money to ruthless tricksters in return for their reversing some fundamental principles of being, for imparting the extremes of lewd experience to children, thus robbing them of childhood and poisoning them with a psychobiological excess for which another payment is still to come. And what about a professor of child & family studies at the University of Syracuse who, in a book published by the New York Times Book Co. and entitled *The Teen-age Survival Book*, writes that a girl, when approached for sex, should ask the boy to use a prophylactic, saying: "All the boys I know enjoy it with a condom on. What's wrong with you?" The professor, in his bottomless stupidity, seems unaware that he teaches whorishness, but his vision of things sexual are reverently published by *New York Times*, the liberal oracle. It's very doubtful that the same organ would publish a rebuke to the phenomenon of professors who, their intentions notwithstanding, actually scavenge on human vulnerabilities. What do we do with the fact that America is the only society in mankind's history in which a publication called *Counterspy—Covert Action Information Bulletin* openly and precisely identifies American intelligence agents—that is, defenders of our freedom against America's most implacable enemy, the Soviet Union— thereby acting in open complicity with that enemy? We could talk about literature, which turned into a slimy retailing of private secretions relentlessly made public and is still stubbornly proclaimed literature by the bull horns of the liberal culture in magazines, electronic media, the daily press.

However, what's called social issues and, in fact, are everyday quandaries of how to live, seem to me of overriding importance. The last Presidential elections were said to be won by President Reagan on pocket-book issues. I have often wondered what, in the end, really motivated the vote of an American working man who was told by his union that Reagan's victory would mean economic policies which would cause the loss of his job, house, two cars and lower-middle-class status, but whose 14-year-old daughter was pregnant while his 16-year-old son was hospitalized for a drug overdose that had crippled his brain for life. Does the man think only in categories of economic well-being, or is there something else that predicates his balloting? After all, he reads the papers, where he learns that one out of six births is now out of wedlock. He only dimly envisions what it means in terms of human misery; yet he connotes what such a mass of children deprived of any normal parental arrangement can mean to the way he himself lives and how he wants his children to live. Furthermore, as he grimly ruminates over his daughter's lot, he must ask himself *why* there are over a million unwanted pregnancies a year among early teen-agers, one consequence of which is that children give birth to often retarded or physiologically damaged infants, irrevocably destroying their own lives by producing new, defective lives. And he must ask himself why, before sex education became mandatory in the high schools, there was seldom such misfortune, and when it did occur it was considered tragic. Today intellectual felons known as doctors and professors whom he sees on TV talk shows advocate sex education for children in spite of statistics that, with every passing year, prove that the already-catastrophic situation is getting worse. But the man's paper that brings him these figures is a liberal paper and does not give him the truth about causes, while there is a Presidential candidate out there who notices the same things he has noticed, and talks about doing something about it. The candidate calls it social issues, and unfortunately forgets about them once he is elected, after he is surrounded by so-called political sophisticates who tell him that those issues are not politically profitable. This, of course, is pure gibberish. Those issues are permanent; addressing them means recognition of reality, thus a more profound participation of politics in human lives. They fuel passions, while the functionalism of economic issues commands only a Pavlovian response. They are the same old, big questions of how to live, on which Moses, Christ, Socrates, Confucius, St. Augustine and others painfully pondered, and which made them humble and established them as mankind's great teachers.

Andrei Tarkowski, a Russian film director with dissident tendencies, once made a movie which was banned by Soviet censorship. The picture begins with a scene in which a 22-year-old man stands at the grave of his father, who had fallen in World War II. The man whispers to himself: "Father, life is so difficult. How to live?" Surrealistically, a voice comes from the grave and says something like: "How can I tell you? When I died, I was just twenty..." A multitude of interpretations can derive from this allegory. We may dismiss the initial question as pompously banal, typical for 19th-century Russian literature. We Westerners have a tradition of inquiring of our philosophical mentors not about how to live but about who to be. During our century psychology, that allegedly hippest of all sciences, became the undisputed compendium of that knowledge, dispenser of preordained attitudes and conditioner of mass-marketed choices. Therefore, there is something naively poignant in that voice from the realm of death, which informs the questioner that one man's concept of how to live was to perish in defense of his country. Above all, there is in both the question and the figurative answer the everlasting craving for rectitude and moral order, as socially valid now as ever, even in our America of liberal nihilism and the Behavioral Left. Hitler won over the German masses by falsely presenting his philosophy as one of moral purity set against Weimar's cynical paradise in which sexual degeneracy and deviation threatened to destroy the very sense of life. We know how nazism perverted that quest for cleansing the collective mind. We in America are heirs to a much more complex civilization whose renewal is possible not through post-Nietzschean, brutalized impulses but through the support of ancient philosophies that have never failed to nourish archhuman needs.

But we should never forget that the masses will not wait forever for the restoration of a guidance for how to live better. The masses can sense that the disintegration of a society begins with the demise of idealism and convention, with the disappearance of distinctions between what's proper and improper, becoming and unbecoming. The working-class mother knows better than a Fifth Avenue socialite that teaching masturbation and orgasm to 12-year-old girls in order to make them "healthier and freer" is an iniquitous sham which spawns a monstrous wilderness of instincts, misdeeds and outrage around us.

That mother cannot verbalize that rearing children on moral fairy tales is better and saner than feeding them a vicious naturalism disguised as innocence: we must do it for her—we who see through the grubbiness of what the liberals and their intellectual mercenaries today call American culture. We are able to debunk the new myths, which are infinitely more mendacious and pernicious than the old ones. There is moral and cultural sophistication in almost every antiliberal and antinihilist proposition against the fakery of freedom unmodified by any normative morality—only the news about it is suppressed, evicted from the pages of the mechanisms of disinformation, centralized in the liberal media, by willful concealment of any alternative. To be sure, we make mistakes which facilitate the fight against us. We have attacked the permissive sexual ethos only in terms of its destruction of arbitrary morals, only as the dissolution of religion, family, the structures of law and order. But what about human feelings and sexual sentiments of a higher order than quantitative competition? What about existential traps and malaises of license? Patriotism, church and the threat of socialism are not the only arguments against promiscuity, and they may even be the weakest ones. Do it or don't is an abstract commandment that won't work; as a matter of fact, it has never worked. Only when it is linked to an individual sense of a rewarding life does it make sense and, in this light, monogamy can be debated not only as ideal but also as a spiritual transaction, a psychomoral comfort: one must perceive a recompense in it to follow it. It is within the territory of refined emotions where the final battle of a regenerated, healthy and moral society will take place. And that is where we have the best chance to win it. Can we still win it? As my most trusted American philosopher, Fats Waller, used to say, "One never knows, do one?"

CHAPTER 18

On Interpretation*

1

Whether you are a corporation or a businessman, you are facing a complex and formidable threat to your existence. It is a menace the typical businessman is only dimly aware of, and even more confused by. He confronts an enemy who has long been waging a war against him, using weapons that are often invisible, or unintelligible to him. He knows his adversaries' faces in politics and union-management conflicts. But there is also an enemy nested in philosophical positions which lie outside the scope of the businessman's natural interests. And his future depends on understanding both those positions and interests.

Many people, influenced by shrill theories, refuse to believe that there is a moral connection in a businessman's soul. Some businesspeople may still nurse the *laissez-faire* machismo that equates moral quandary with economic weakness. But I see the contemporary businessman as an embattled and struggling species. This condition makes him more enlightened and sensitive than both his predecessors and his detractors. He is now a sort of resistance movement fighter, deeply perturbed by the appalling discrepancy between the actual value of what he accomplishes and the common assessment of his efforts by the hostile commentators. In spite of the contempt for his personality and goals which his enemies have been fanning for over a century, he still sees the real import of his activities and a legitimate harmony between his personal satisfactions and his practical achievements. Even if in his heart he has the honesty to admit that acquisitiveness, or cupidity, is not alien to him, that acknowledgment does not diminish the belief that he is doing something right, something reflected in society's well-being. At the same time, he notices at each step that his usefulness is unrecognized, and often rejected. He is correct in wanting appreciation, as he objectively enriches and improves his social reality.

An updated shortcut through history shows that the modern businessman has not only been shaped by economic and social factors, as Marxists of all hues insist, but also has been formed and circumscribed by cultural factors —ideas, propensities, attitudes and desires. The Western world's economic productivity has always been intermingled with the blossoming of philosophical and religious concepts, spiritual and moral advancement, political and social doctrines. Theorists have never been able to agree on what comes first: the socioeconomic arrangements, or the prescriptions on how to live, work, behave, love, pray, produce and distribute. Whether empiricism,

*This essay was delivered in part as a lecture during the Rockford College Institute's Corporate Responsibility Seminar on June 2, 1978.

rationalism or positivism hatched the bourgeois, and formed his ideas and virtues, or whether he, industrious and victorious, begot these philosophies, is less important than the fact that his consistent support of values, virtues and ideals has made capitalistic civilizations thrive, and has made life in them more humane than anywhere else. The essential element, free enterprise, gave rise to the modern businessman, and he owes no apology to anyone for who he is. Capitalism is among mankind's crucial discoveries, and it is its own warrant for an improved future, if it can survive the cultural assault.

2

Some time ago, Yale University focused attention upon this conflict, devoting an entire issue of the *Yale Alumni Magazine* to the interplay between capitalism and culture. The Yale authors observed that after Karl Marx had identified capitalism as the foe of all goodness, Western scholars and intellectuals orchestrated his theme eventually bringing general disfavor to this economic system in the eyes of Western societies. The century-long crescendo of castigation has been a peculiar phenomenon inasmuch as these scholars and intellectuals who have been so forceful in their enmity have incomparable liberty and prosperity under the very free market system which they condemn. Capitalism has supplied them with the freedom of speech, the good food, the access to sports and games, the scientific research unbridled by any moral limitations, the well-tailored tweed jackets, the comfortable political security, and the means to promulgate their recipes for universal salvation, even when these were aimed at the destruction of capitalism itself. What the Yale professors chose not to confront is the role played by envy and the desire for power. To my mind, the magnetic appeal which Marxian theory has had for intellectuals is best explainable in terms of a rising class of intelligentsia which craved political power and envied the capitalists' ability to provide the people with tangible goods, not merely theories. What they hated was the image of the businessman as the provisioner of the cornucopia, which had been entrenched in the common folk awareness since the Italian Renaissance. Envy and the will to power would seem to be the cause for them to attack that image and dream up a socialist state in which idealistic economists and sanctimonious bureaucrats could supplant businessmen and provide people with bread, cloth and shelter. The results, from Lenin on, are all around.

The incontestable merit of the Yale report on the state of capitalism is not in its tepid acquiescence that capitalism is not altogether without merits. It is in its recognition that capitalism's eventual renascence will not come from its objective superiority, but from refurbishing its image. Capitalism, both as a system and a way of life, must be reevaluated and reinterpreted with the help of primarily noneconomic criteria.

3

Most defenders of capitalism today, the fiery and the temperate alike, have concluded that if only people understood how logically capitalism works when not obstructed by intervention and encroachment, it would gain their devotion and could be freed once again to perform miracles. The point is valid, but not useful, for it assumes that the problems of anticapitalism are subject to rational resolution, that when truth and its proper interpretation are generally understood, political remedies will follow. The dogmatic practices of using federal revenues to restructure the society became routine with Roosevelt and the New Deal. Since that time some 70 foundations have been created whose central goal is to make known to the American people the beautiful mechanism of the market, but the Golden Age of idyllic love between business and society has not resulted. Business, as a social institution, and the businessman, as its practitioner and missionary, are more vilified than ever. This is where the misinterpretation, or, actually, the notion of interpretation, requires some explanation. Since the media, which now have an effective monopoly on the interpretations of what happens in our time, society, and the world at large, have successively transformed themselves from reporters about power into power brokers, and, finally, into a rapacious and virtually unrestrained power in its own right, they became the ultimate weapon in the hands of the intellectual class. To protect this dominion, the intelligentsia has to have a moral rationale for its preponderance. Hence, the inaccurate claim that the press is an agent of enlightenment, whose moral mission is to safeguard the "people's right to know." However, it has been repeatedly demonstrated that we have not been receiving full and balanced knowledge under their implementation of our right to know, restricted as it is by *their* decisions about what we *should* know, or what they *want* us to know. The means of selecting the information presented by the press lords is quite murky. Theirs is an arbitrary choice which, in the end, limits our knowledge, and consequently forms our concepts of social duty. They demand unconditional trust in *their* opinion, in *their* probity and moral intentions. Thus, *their* interpretations of news and information become the supreme norm of our knowledge. Too often, those interpretations turn out to be calculated manipulations of our views and our priorities. Having cast themselves as the watchdog of faith, conduct and politics, they seldom admit that they also have the power to discredit faith, prescribe conduct and cause political events.

4

According to Webster's Dictionary, to *interpret* means to bring out meanings not immediately apparent. Throughout history, those who were called upon to interpret — the sages, priests, philosophers, and ideologists — have recognized that interpreting could influence minds and create facts.

Today interpretation has been refined to a high art in which partisanship, advocacy and promotion are presented and increasingly accepted as an objective explanation. Interpretation, thus has become the all-purpose tool to sway beliefs. Television has produced an even more frightening interpretative dimension which Daniel Boorstin has identified as the "crisis of human consciousness." We have reached the point where reality is not necessarily what's real and true, but what is interpreted for us as reality by the various cultural institutions, the universities, the print and broadcast media and the entertainment industry. A claim can be made that it has always been so, that the cultural agents have only replaced one another, and that all that's really changed is the technology. "It ain't necessarily so..." as Sporting Life said in "Porgy and Bess." Through the ages, truth has always been a difficult, but nevertheless concrete concept. With the advent of the totalitarian philosophies of the nineteenth century, like Marxism, "truths" made their debut. Which truth is better and which worse was to be made known to the people through interpretation. Fast printing processes, mass-production, mass distribution, the radio, the movie industry, and finally TV have made the interpretation of ideas into a formidable weapon when they are dominated by a single ideology. The same was valid for political facts. The Pentagon Papers had no informative importance, the news in them was outdated, their details known. They had no political clout. The liberal position, long championed by the press, was a hands-down winner, the issue a foregone conclusion. The government opposed their publication on the grounds that it would be dangerously detrimental to the authority of the republic to reward with fame and respectability a disloyal official who, for either shady or idealistic purposes, felt free to steal state documents and abuse the public trust vested in him. The press claimed that it had the absolute right to decide what could and should be published in this country. Midway through the struggle, it became clear that all that mattered to the press was to have its will enforced, while the pious slogans about its "freedom" and the "people's right to know" were used to assure it the support of Americans for its "righteous" fight.

Only a few people realize that the media's dominance of interpretation enables them to shape popular attitudes and values. In the past, this power to form and influence public beliefs into patterns which are now called lifestyles, resided in religion, education, arts and letters, Mores were shaped by ideas borne in more judicious quarters than gossip columns. Today even the best child after prolonged and ubiquitous exposure to distorted Freudism, as it is pushed by the media, becomes a bad child. *Parade,* an allegedly family-oriented Sunday supplement in many American newspapers, informs on demand about who lives with whom, for how long, and with what sexual preferences. This kind of information is not meant as a recounting of the facts of life, but as a stamp of approval, easily detectable in the tone of the reporting itself. Naturally, it finds followers by the millions — so that in our time the so-called "sexual liberation" rather than being a massive natural phenomenon, has been popularized and multiplied by the press for reasons known only to itself. Irving Lazar, America's mightiest literary agent, divulged not long ago the secret of creating an impact for a book; he said: "The whole point is getting books on the front pages of newspapers..." Which amounts to saying that had the *New York Times,* or *Washington Post* for ideological reasons, taken a dislike to Montaigne, Defoe, Dostoyevsky or Melville, they would never have made it on their own merit. For the same reason a Norman Mailer, a Joan Didion, a Gore Vidal and a Lillian Hellman, who propagate a morally crippled America, have been fabricated by the press into symbols of high culture, demigods and mythical exemplars.

Interpretation can, of course, be used in many innovative ways. All of these submethods are labeled with marvelous euphemisms. Pressure groups and factions, notwithstanding their ofttimes brutal and totalitarian disregard for the rights of others, are constantly pushed into public view because, according to the media newspeak, they are "newsworthy." This means that the media reward their crass shrillness with publicity, regardless of the message. Hippiedom, feminism, terrorism, the pseudo-revolution of the '60s, and the trumpeted sexual limbo of the '70s continuously occupy center stage, for they are meretricious issues. The so-called "smart" groups know their attractiveness in the media age. By backing them initially for commercial sensationalism, the media wind up supporting their causes, becoming more or less advocates of their morality, or immorality, philosophy or idiocy. Supporting not what's good but what's loud and aggressive is specious power-brokerage, but the power of interpretation can easily deal with its inconveniences. All they need do is repeat something often enough confusing millions and bolstering their own supremacy amidst the public confusion and contention.

When we enter the realm of television we can easily see the heightened distortion of interpretation. TV has brought a new fascination; it seems to transform any event — even the most evil and ugly ones — into uncanny propaganda for itself, for those who perpetrated or enacted it. It is hard to pinpoint how one of mankind's most miraculous inventions has rendered to it such a tragic disservice. Perhaps it is because depicting evil does not reduce its spread, or annihilate it, but instead makes it more respectable and acceptable. Or maybe because when people are engaged in imagining the suffering by reading novels, or watching its imitation onstage, they become more charitable, whereas by following photographed reality they lose their potential for compassion and become indifferent to it —making the modern terrorist so cruel and contemptuous of any humanness. TV as an industry and medium has decided not to be bothered by this problem. Boorstin, the distinguished Librarian of Congress, calls TV an "ally of hijackers" and asks: "Can we survive the transformation of experience which television has brought us?" It will be difficult. Especially in the light of the enunciation by the director of ABC News who said in an interview: "Television's right to report is indeed absolute." He was echoed by a colleague from CBS who went even further:

"It's always better to report than not to report...if we thought at any time that life was endangered...as a direct result of our reporting, *our policy* permits us to delay the story..." Which shows that human life, these days, depends on a TV network's *policy* as the supreme determinant. We have already had tragic proof of how this TV credo works in the society at large: CBS was repeatedly warned that its notorious Charles Manson documentary had the potential to generate the worst kind of violence; ignoring all warnings, they aired it in Chicago in 1977, and soon afterwards a Manson-like slaughter took place in Illinois, the murderer admitting that he was inspired by the TV show. "Humans assimilate what they see," said Henri Bergson, a French philosopher, decades before the advent of TV; we can safely add today: we *are* what we see. We also know *only* what we see, which opens the way for TV's sponsorship of endless massacres of knowledge through interpretative distortions. In 1969, numerous events which attempted to dismantle American universities were shown, but a rally of nearly 100,000 students in Miami, Florida, who opposed radicalism, was not.

5

Capitalism is a manifestation of common sense, while anticapitalism is a rejection of common sense. Common sense is the arch enemy of interpretations founded in sophistry. Common sense opposes freedom without authority and responsibility. It resists the enforced brotherhood of nonconsenting adults, rejects obvious distortions of reality, denies that standards of living can be raised by guaranteeing wages unrelated to productivity. The person committed to the salutary force of common sense will never understand the liberal's slander of the "ruthless" food industry which, over the last century, has dramatically increased the longevity of Americans and improved their health and teeth, making our nation the envy of the rest of the world.

There are few more trenchant examples of the abuse of common sense than the liberal-journalistic interpretation of capitalism. How often does the mass media glorify the achievements of capitalism? When and where has the business community been described with terms like "excellence," "boon," "inventiveness," or "good will"? Capitalism's success and virtues are not considered newsworthy by the media, whereas capitalism's mistakes, transgressions and misfortunes make up the bulk of domestic news and are seized upon with relish in the liberal media interpretations. The liberal culture's interpretation of capitalism is marked by blatant paradoxes that should be of prime concern to the American business community, but unfortunately are not. The term "transvestite capitalism" correctly describes the essence of the most damaging contradiction. That same liberal who feels free to blast the American system of moral and economic values for engendering vile inequalities, does it most often from a Fifth Avenue condominium, Hollywood mansion, or a chauffeured Rolls-Royce, and nobody sees either the knavishness or the insolence in it. It would be only a slight exaggeration to claim that the most formidable adversary of American business is wealth. Is this a paradox? Maybe, but it is the sort which has the potency to tear at the commonsensical fabric of our lives and cause far-reaching social malaises. Wealth mobilized against business is to be seen most clearly in the multibillion dollar rock music industry whose psychosocial message includes the evils of the inhumane society created by capitalism and its vices: a rock star today spouts his vituperant anticapitalistic pseudopoetry to the tune of six figures per show. "Rock and roll is a way of life," writes Robert Stephen Spitz in his book *The Making of a Superstar.* "It has given us new heroes, new thoughts and philosophies through well-constructed lyrics..." The calamity of our time is that no one in the American media asks: Who are these new heroes? What do they want? What are their thoughts, philosophies and lyrics, and what will their moral and social consequences be? However, as Mr. Sptiz reports, "Excess earnings, made from extraordinary rock profits, are cautiously counseled into shrewd investments by staid Wall Street banking houses that, only years earlier, spurned its bankability. Today, rock music is considered one of the most stable and durable industries, and those same banking houses have even gone as far as to place their own capital behind managers' and artists' existing contracts in an attempt to gain a quick return on their investment." Here begins a vicious circle of fateful dimension. The American civilization has for many years vaunted its elasticity: it can be pulled apart by disruptive forces, but it is never torn asunder. It survives explosions and erosions, absorbs diseases and afflictions and miraculously turns them into fertilizers as rebellious generations mellow into quiet contributors to the development process. But of late, this formerly infallible quality reveals fissures. Common sense — this civilization's marrow — no longer seems to be able to rise to the surface. The following is a quote by a certain Edward Sorel, a radical, left-wing political cartoonist: "For the past fifteen years, I've been making cartoons that in one way or another suggest that America is educated by incompetents, governed by hypocrites, and ruled by the military-industrial complex. In spite of this anarchistic proselytizing, my alma mater has given me its highest award, the Senate has requested my art for permanent exhibition, and in two weeks Random House, a wholly-owned subsidiary of RCA, is publishing *Superpen,* a collection of my cartoons." Many will say, that's exactly what makes America victorious and noble: criticism is permitted, tolerated and sustained. And it would be to this civilization's credit if it could prove that such toleration has a self-cleansing and self-improving effect. But it no longer does. Hostility is in the driver's seat. Capitalism's embrace of criticism is now dismantling capitalism, one of this civilization's fundamental premises, and rewarding Mr. Sorel for planting a cancerous tissue that eats away at RCA, who has turned Mr. Sorel into a wealthy man for spitting into their eye and trying to destroy them. No one knows how to deal with the muddle of transvestite capitalism, and, actually, no one wishes to. So the capitalists continue to destroy themselves, and instead of being applauded for it, receive even more insults from their assailants. Many capitalists, however, seem to venerate their own humiliation and adore their condemners. They seem to feel that financing their ideological foes is a gesture full of democratic virtue and cultural sophistication.

6

What does the corporate advertiser get for the money he pays? Does he get merely the desired space on a page, or prime time on the air, to promote his product or services? Or does he get something more? Or less?

As things stand now, he gets less. He contributes to the very existence of a paper or network, which is generally against him and everything he stands for, devotes his life to and banks his future on. None of the powerful liberal media organs will admit, as does the radical press, that its intention is the elimination of American capitalism, but most of them never cease defending and supporting causes, groups and events which openly serve that goal. However, it would be difficult to find in the *New York Times, Newsweek* or any NBC program a statement unequivocally proclaiming that capitalism is good, and should be protected and supported because it constitutes this country's asset and pride.

This is enough of a reason for any corporate advertiser to urgently concern himself with the substance of what is published or broadcast by the medium in which he advertises. As a matter of fact, it's not only his business but his duty, as the media interpret information according to liberal dogma, which in most instances means a definite antibusiness slant. Thus, from the perspective of business, what is at stake is not tolerance, freedom of opinions, independence of inquiry, even simple democratic fairness — which are so blatantly refused to the business community — but the survival of capitalism. It is the corporation's responsibility to disprove the image of the prototypical grasping egotist, so painstakingly affixed to the business community by the intelligentsia. This image has been painted in arts and letters for more than a century, depicting the businessman as unable to justify his existence and endeavors except through a craving for profits and vulgar materialism. What the corporate executive, a modern, highly trained college graduate, has in common with this obsolete cliche, is hard to see, but the cliche persists, sustained by liberal scorn and hostility. Not before businesspeople begin to ask sharp, pertinent questions and demand intellectual satisfaction from their critics can this image be disposed of. Then the human face of capitalism —that aspect which is larger than the mechanism of the free market — can reappear in American culture.

The shedding of the image will be futile, however, if it means embracing the fashionable proliberal incoherences and snobberies. Some time ago, aboard a United Airlines plane, I reached for the house magazine entitled *Mainliner.*

There, I found an article by Mr. Richard Ferris, the carrier's president, who poignantly complained about the government's overregulations and interventions; his was followed by articles by an anticapitalistic historian Mr. Henry Steele Commager, and by a procommunist journalist, Ms. Frances Fitz-Gerald. I wrote to Mr. Ferris expressing sympathy with his troubles, and surprise at finding his arch enemies in his own publication. I added that though the subject matter of Mr. Commager's and Ms. FitzGerald's articles were remote from the private airline industry, in the long run they are lethal for its *raison d'etre;* and as such, they should at least be balanced by other views. I soon received a reply from Mr. Ferris' deputy for public affairs who wrote: "The primary purpose of *Mainliner* is to inform and entertain our passengers, not to convert them to our philosophy or ideology." A dignified answer to be sure, but dangerously stupid and ultimately irresponsible. To an unprejudiced mind "informing" implies exactly what I postulated, namely evenhandedness in the attention to major public issues. I have continued to scan *Mainliner* on my travels and have found a predominance of leftists, radicals, and modish liberal pseudoauthorities in its pages. *Mainliner,* in contrast to what the management of United Airlines thinks and believes in, has been farmed out to people who perform only according to their own beliefs and commitments.

7

What business needs today in America is a thoughtfully assembled body of ideas which would bring out its *cultural* image. When Dow Chemical refused to continue to subsidize a university that paid Jane Fonda thousands of dollars for a virulent anticorporate lecture — its decision was labeled mind control and it was accused of a grave abuse of academic freedom. When the ERA militants try to extort votes through an economic boycott this is called a legitimate weapon. Both cases exemplify capitalism's cultural defenselessness.

I dined not long ago with an NBC international correspondent, a bright young man whose star is rising, who quite correctly grieved over contemporary malaises and sores. When asked who should be blamed for them, he delivered the routine attack on callous American materialism, the natural offshoot of the free enterprise system. My suggestion that perhaps communism could be a remedy he vehemently rejected. I thus asked him what he would propose after dismissing both systems. "That is not my business," he answered.

His may not be the classical liberal stance, but it is a telling one. As for us, the partisans of common sense, we know that no economic arrangement is all wine and roses, but it is our business to look for and support the better one. We also know that a young NBC journalist can freely exercise his profession, indulge in his freedom of convictions, and enjoy a high salary only because America is still a free capitalistic country. Thus, what the young man actually demands is the luxury of biting off the hand that feeds him, while projecting his·unconcern for replacing it with any other device. His shallow intellectual preferences and frustrations he deems a profundity of mind and feeling. It might be that in this shortsighted insouciance lies our greatest chance.

The liberals in both the media and higher education exhort American business to provide financial support for them without examining what goals are served by these two enormously influential institutions. They say: "Trust us! You don't have any business looking into what we publish, broadcast and teach. We are trained to know what's right or wrong. We have an exclusive franchise on deciding what's best for society, also for you. By trusting us, you are helping mankind and its ideals." But, on closer scrutiny, it seems that neither the press, nor the universities can bring themselves to affirm that capitalism's endeavors may be beneficial to mankind. So, why trust them?

CHAPTER 19

Accentuate the Negative*

I am most often accused of two venial sins: liberal-baiting and negativism. Of course, both charges have the common rockbottom. I concentrate on liberal culture because it is the reigning sociocultural sovereign whose wisdom and morality I question and challenge. Caring for values of intellect and literary excellence, I unfortunately have little to point out as satisfactory answers to the lib-cultural dominance. Whenever I run across them in fiction, arts or humanities, I praise them to the skies. However, as there are not enough of them of the quality I would wholeheartedly approve, I am often accused of sounding negative by my own brethren in *Weltanschauung*.

This, certainly, is a comedy of errors. I need not go back to Roger Williams to try to explain negativism and give it a fair and reasonable interpretation. What happened in the '50s will do. It was a time of economic prosperity in America, not unmarred, but serene, social moods, slow but steady progress of American humanitarianism, steady improvements in civil rights at home, and of American moral authority abroad. Liberals, especially their radical variation, did not like it at all. Through complicated sociocultural processes, they succeeded in instilling in a good part of the enlightened strata a feeling of distrust and contempt for the social truce, for the healthy, if simplistic, anticommunism and anticollectivism of the masses, for the sentiments of satisfaction with the well-justified patriotism. They began to negate the American values. They went victoriously into the '60s and declared America, as Americans knew her, an abyss of dimwitted complacency, a plastic wasteland of moral stupor and ticky-tacky existence. This was negativism at its best (or worst). It started the bizarre belly dancing of the American liberal intellectual, which has continued for roughly a quarter of a century to the point of negativistic irrationalism. The tradition of Western civilization holds that there is nothing wrong with the critique of one's society or country, provided we all stick to some criteria of reasonableness and normalcy. The rest of the world saw in America a better reality; the liberal radicals saw in it a worse reality—such a discrepancy has produced a glut of stale lies, useless but rabid moral cliches and social pseudoremedies. Once they became institutionalized by the liberal culture and its media, a movement toward their exposure and purification was inevitable. And it's here where my negativism comes in: I feel compelled to negate the pernicious negation of America.

From today's perspective, we clearly see how the manic rage against

*Editorial in *Chronicles of Culture*, January/February 1979. (Vol. 3, No. 1)

America — its ethos and food and traditions and purpose — became a viral disease of both the nations' body and soul. The fashion of branding as corruption and vice anything the mind of a liberal abhorred turned into an affliction of everyday process of living. When all primary truths became twisted by the grossly subjectivist perceptions of writers, gurus, theorists, *et alii.* who, in addition, knew how to turn their hatred of America into a most profitable profession, the wholesome vectors of society were quickly obliterated. One could see protesters who fiercely demanded the right to protest while they, without bar or hindrance, shouted their protests in the streets in broad daylight; this was conceived as and called an act of noble liberation of the collective mind, which amounts to the same level of brain power as calling a tree a bird. However, the media at large sustained such a falsification of the reality. It left me with no choice but to negate such "truth" and "fact" and "reality," and prodded me to sift through the ravages of the torn fabric of American common sense, normalcy, and understanding of the basics of being. It is, perhaps, why now, when I openly reject a lie, I am reproached for being obsessed with negativism by those who still feel more comfortable with glittering fantasies than with the decency of unassailable and factual evidence.

To try to trace the enmity between their negativism and my negation of it, I would have to chart the interplay between the liberal worldview and mine, and outline the points which induce me to firm resistance and rejection. Let's take spiritual fairness. I have never accused the liberals of evil intentions, only of intellectual error which leads to distorted moral judgment. The danger of the liberal culture is especially poignant. This cultural pattern maximizes the camouflaged totalitarianism inherent in the liberal persuasion; as touted from every page of the press, it denies moral legitimacy, or even positiveness, to any of my ideological attitudes. My economic beliefs are decried as rooted in greed, my social and moral philosophy is, to a liberal, a product of antihuman alienation, thus condemnable in advance without hearing. The foundation of liberal individualism is the faith in the perfectability of man — a high-minded presumption but nevertheless disputable; this blind trust gives the American liberal a peculiar odor of saintliness, frantically diffused by the media all over America throughout the last half a century. A liberal believes that evil is automatically accumulated by tradition, stability and the mere history of social relations; anyone who attempts to contradict this fallacy is branded an enemy. I do not consider myself an enemy of liberals, I only negate their patterns of thinking — and this is enough for liberals to see me as an enemy. Curiously enough, some people of good will and intelligence, who perceive the liberal self-deception, still do not consider my exposure of this deception a help to our fellow man, but an unbecoming, aggressive negativism.

Though the liberals sincerely oppose communism and the political totalitarianism of the left, they somehow, oddly, see in it not evil, but aberration. But they do perceive wickedness and horror in the totalitarian movements of the right. I do not quarrel with that, but I must vehemently reject the special moral tariff accorded the ideological thugs and hoodlums whom the Marxian sacraments exempt, in the eyes of a liberal, from moral proscription. However, if politics and economy still serve as a meeting ground where my rejection has a chance to hold its own against his negation — in culture, the liberal has become a menace. He operates with impunity as an unmasked totalitarian and a supra-negativist, one who has managed, in the space of two decades, to destroy the entire universe of ethical restraints and behavioral conventions by which the Western civilization has lived and thrived for two millenia. But he not only eliminates rationality and rectitude from the cultural ebb and tide, he also insists that accentuating the negative has a salutary and auspicious value. Value-free mass culture, the liberal culture's end goal, like value-free pop culture, mass eduction and mass art, is a contradiction in terms. Value-free art has always existed, but by definition it must be exclusive and hermetic, an ivory tower probe into artistic dimensions devoid of social significance. Once this principle is transgressed, havoc is wrought upon individual lives and societies. What's popular must be value-oriented not only to be art, but chiefly to perform the one and only acceptable *social* function of art, culture, education. This, a liberal negates, and I most solemnly negate his negation.

I have also been chided by some for my preoccupation with what I call the liberal establishment, and to which I ascribe a lot of nasty habits. But I stand by my notion, and here it is fitting to say that it is exactly that liberal establishment which enforces the circumstances described above, and imposes them on America. Let's try to clarify this point.

My critics maintain that by speaking of an establishment I imply a sort of conspiracy, which is a construct of my imagination. But is it really so? When I speak of an establishment, I imply the existence of others, for only in democracies do they exist; in a totalitarian country, there's only *one* establishment, and that's it. In America, we have many establishments, among them the liberal establishment that rules the culture. However, when the banking establishment is attacked, the attackers rarely suggest conspiracy; the alleged sins of bankers are too visible for their detractors to sniff a plot. Neither do I suggest that the liberal establishment runs the American culture by means of conspiratorial cabals and tricks, by tight organizational methods and orders issued from an anonymous center of decision. I recognize that the liberal establishment is simply using the oldest, most reliable and lethal tool of oppression which has always been used by reigning establishments to operate the mechanism of control — namely fashion. It's the terrorism of fashionable ideas that gives the liberal establishment its power. I most forcefully negate this sway and will do whatever I can to assist in comprehending this establishment and join in its condemnation. As long as liberals make careers of negating what is good and propitious, for that long will I be negating their negativism in order to bring about a new sense of affirmation.